Kaplan Publishing are constantly finding new ways to support students looking for exam success and our online resources really do add an extra dimension to your studies.

This book comes with free MyKaplan online resources so that you can study anytime, anywhere. **This free online resource is not sold separately and is included in the price of the book.**

Having purchased this book, you have access to the following online study materials:

CONTENT	AAT	
	Text	Kit
Electronic version of the book	✓	✓
Knowledge Check tests with instant answers	✓	
Mock assessments online	✓	✓
Material updates	✓	✓

How to access your online resources

Received this book as part of your Kaplan course?
If you have a MyKaplan account, your full online resources will be added automatically, in line with the information in your course confirmation email. If you've not used MyKaplan before, you'll be sent an activation email once your resources are ready.

Bought your book from Kaplan?
We'll automatically add your online resources to your MyKaplan account. If you've not used MyKaplan before, you'll be sent an activation email.

Bought your book from elsewhere?
Go to **www.mykaplan.co.uk/add-online-resources**
Enter the ISBN number found on the title page and back cover of this book.
Add the unique pass key number contained in the scratch panel below.
You may be required to enter additional information during this process to set up or confirm your account details.

This code can only be used once for the registration of this book online. This registration and your online content will expire when the examinations covered by this book have taken place. Please allow one hour from the time you submit your book details for us to process your request.

Please scratch the film to access your unique code.

Please be aware that this code is case-sensitive and you will need to include the dashes within the passcode, but not when entering the ISBN.

PRINCIPLES OF BOOKKEEPING CONTROLS

STUDY TEXT

Qualifications and Credit Framework

Q2022

This Study Text supports study for the following AAT qualifications:

AAT Level 2 Certificate in Accounting

AAT Level 2 Certificate in Bookkeeping

AAT Certificate in Accounting at SCQF Level 6

KAPLAN PUBLISHING'S STATEMENT OF PRINCIPLES

LINGUISTIC DIVERSITY, EQUALITY AND INCLUSION

We are committed to diversity, equality and inclusion and strive to deliver content that all users can relate to.

We are here to make a difference to the success of every learner.

Clarity, accessibility and ease of use for our learners are key to our approach.

We will use contemporary examples that are rich, engaging and representative of a diverse workplace.

We will include a representative mix of race and gender at the various levels of seniority within the businesses in our examples to support all our learners in aspiring to achieve their potential within their chosen careers.

Roles played by characters in our examples will demonstrate richness and diversity by the use of different names, backgrounds, ethnicity and gender, with a mix of sexuality, relationships and beliefs where these are relevant to the syllabus.

It must always be obvious who is being referred to in each stage of any example so that we do not detract from clarity and ease of use for each of our learners.

We will actively seek feedback from our learners on our approach and keep our policy under continuous review. If you would like to provide any feedback on our linguistic approach, please use this form (you will need to enter the link below into your browser).

https://forms.gle/U8oR3abiPpGRDY158

We will seek to devise simple measures that can be used by independent assessors to randomly check our success in the implementation of our Linguistic Equality, Diversity and Inclusion Policy.

PRINCIPLES OF BOOKKEEPING CONTROLS

British Library Cataloguing-in-Publication Data

A catalogue record for this book is available from the British Library.

Published by
Kaplan Publishing UK
Unit 2, The Business Centre
Molly Millars Lane
Wokingham
Berkshire
RG41 2QZ

ISBN: 978-1-83996-870-9

The text in this material and any others made available by any Kaplan Group company does not amount to advice on a particular matter and should not be taken as such. No reliance should be placed on the content as the basis for any investment or other decision or in connection with any advice given to third parties. Please consult your appropriate professional adviser as necessary. Kaplan Publishing Limited and all other Kaplan group companies expressly disclaim all liability to any person in respect of any losses or other claims, whether direct, indirect, incidental, consequential or otherwise arising in relation to the use of such materials.

© Kaplan Financial Limited, 2024

Printed and bound in Great Britain.

All rights reserved. No part of this publication may be reproduced, stored in a retrieval system, or transmitted, in any form or by any means, electronic, mechanical, photocopying, recording or otherwise, without the prior written permission of Kaplan Publishing.

PRINCIPLES OF BOOKKEEPING CONTROLS

CONTENTS

	Page number
Introduction	P.5
Unit guide	P.9
The assessment	P.17
Unit link to the End Point Assessment (EPA)	P.18
Study skills	P.19

STUDY TEXT

Chapter

1	Double-entry bookkeeping	1
2	Control accounts and reconciliations	57
3	Errors and suspense accounts	93
4	Payroll procedures	117
5	The banking system and bank reconciliations	137
Mock Assessment Questions		171
Mock Assessment Answers		189
Appendix 1: International accounting terminology and the alternatives		201
Index		I.1

PRINCIPLES OF BOOKKEEPING CONTROLS

INTRODUCTION

HOW TO USE THESE MATERIALS

These Kaplan Publishing learning materials have been carefully designed to make your learning experience as easy as possible and to give you the best chance of success in your AAT assessments.

They contain a number of features to help you in the study process.

The sections on the Unit Guide, the Assessment and Study Skills should be read before you commence your studies.

They are designed to familiarise you with the nature and content of the assessment and to give you tips on how best to approach your studies.

STUDY TEXT

This study text has been specially prepared for the revised AAT qualification introduced in February 2022.

It is written in a practical and interactive style:

- key terms and concepts are clearly defined

- all topics are illustrated with practical examples with clearly worked solutions based on sample tasks provided by the AAT in the new examining style

- frequent activities throughout the chapters ensure that what you have learnt is regularly reinforced

- 'pitfalls' and 'examination tips' help you avoid commonly made mistakes and help you focus on what is required to perform well in your examination

- 'Test your understanding' activities are included within each chapter to apply your learning and develop your understanding.

ICONS

The chapters include the following icons throughout.

They are designed to assist you in your studies by identifying key definitions and the points at which you can test yourself on the knowledge gained.

 Definition

These sections explain important areas of Knowledge which must be understood and reproduced in an assessment.

 Example

The illustrative examples can be used to help develop an understanding of topics before attempting the activity exercises.

 Test your understanding

These are exercises which give the opportunity to assess your understanding of all the assessment areas.

 Foundation activities

These are questions to help ground your knowledge and consolidate your understanding on areas you're finding tricky.

 Extension activities

These questions are for if you're feeling confident or wish to develop your higher level skills.

Quality and accuracy are of the utmost importance to us so if you spot an error in any of our products, please send an email to mykaplanreporting@kaplan.com with full details.

Our Quality Co-ordinator will work with our technical team to verify the error and take action to ensure it is corrected in future editions.

Progression

There are two elements of progression that we can measure: first how quickly students move through individual topics within a subject, and second how quickly they move from one course to the next. We know that there is an optimum for both, but it can vary from subject to subject and from student to student. However, using data and our experience of student performance over many years, we can make some generalisations.

A fixed period of study set out at the start of a course with key milestones is important. This can be within a subject, for example 'I will finish this topic by 30 June', or for overall achievement, such as 'I want to be qualified by the end of next year'.

Your qualification is cumulative, as earlier papers provide a foundation for your subsequent studies, so do not allow there to be too big a gap between one subject and another.

We know that exams encourage techniques that lead to some degree of short term retention, the result being that you will simply forget much of what you have already learned unless it is refreshed (look up Ebbinghaus Forgetting Curve for more details on this). This makes it more difficult as you move from one subject to another: not only will you have to learn the new subject, you will also have to relearn all the underpinning knowledge as well. This is very inefficient and slows down your overall progression which makes it more likely you may not succeed at all.

In addition, delaying your studies slows your path to qualification which can have negative impacts on your career, postponing the opportunity to apply for higher level positions and therefore higher pay.

PRINCIPLES OF BOOKKEEPING CONTROLS

You can use the following diagram showing the whole structure of your qualification to help you keep track of your progress.

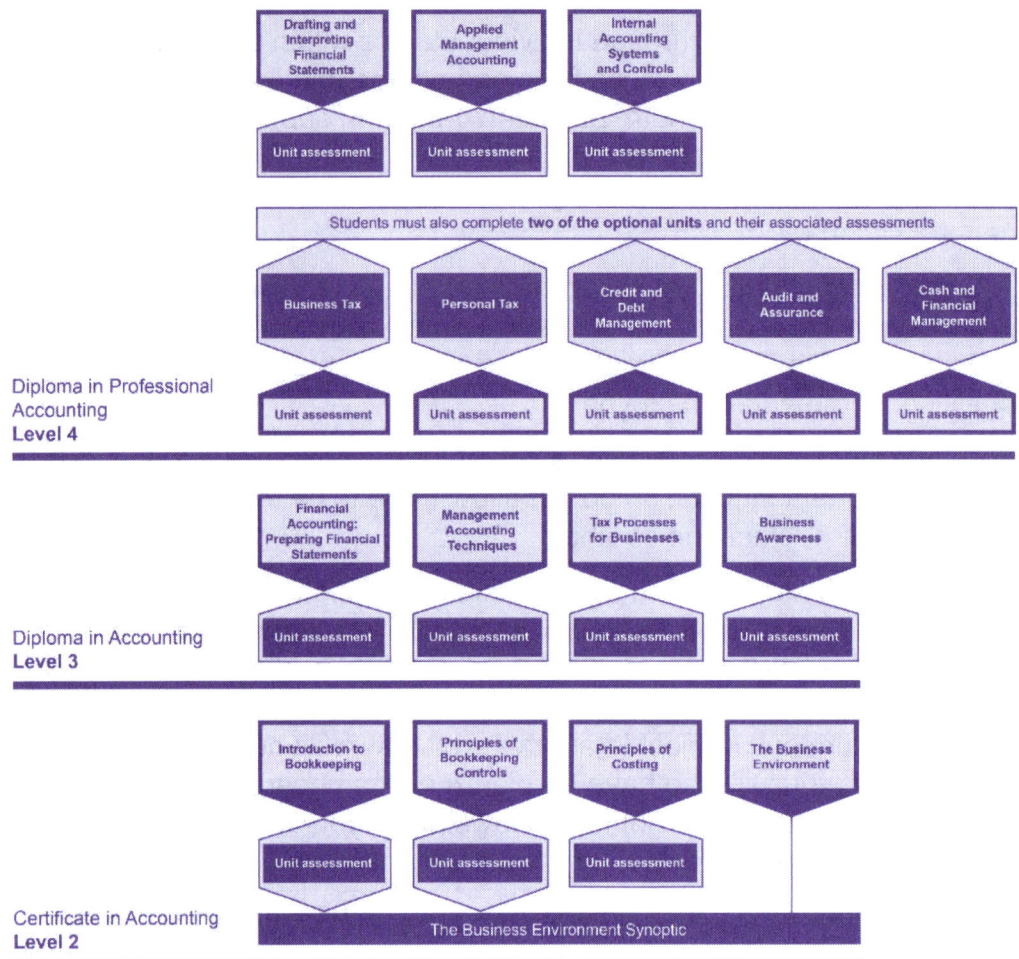

PRINCIPLES OF BOOKKEEPING CONTROLS

UNIT GUIDE

Introduction

This unit builds on the knowledge and skills acquired from studying Introduction to Bookkeeping and explores control accounts, journals and reconciliations. It takes students through a number of processes used in bookkeeping that help verify and validate the entries made. These processes enable the student to understand the purpose of control accounts and associated reconciliations. Students will also understand the use of the journal to the stage of redrafting the trial balance, following initial adjustments.

This unit covers procedures that are required to ensure bookkeeping is completed beyond purely entering or processing initial transactions, which will enable students to develop their understanding of the relationship between the various accounting records and consolidate their knowledge of double-entry bookkeeping.

Students will develop the ability to prepare the value added tax (VAT) control account as well as the receivables and payables ledger control accounts, including reconciliation with the receivables and payables ledgers. They will use the journal to record a variety of transactions, including the correction of errors. Students will be able to redraft the initial trial balance, following adjustments. They will learn to update the cash book following receipt of a bank statement, and also how to prepare a bank reconciliation statement.

This unit explores the knowledge required to complete these bookkeeping procedures both manually and digitally. While the student will not be expected to demonstrate the ability to use any specific accounting software, the unit will explain to them where digital accounting systems are automating processes they are learning. The skills and knowledge gained will enable students to understand the business environment and facilitate their comprehension of a digital accounting system. Reference to digital systems includes applications as well as both desktop and cloud accounting software.

PRINCIPLES OF BOOKKEEPING CONTROLS

Learning outcomes

On completion of this unit the learner will be able to:

- Use control accounts
- Reconcile a bank statement with the cash book
- Use the journal
- Produce trial balances

Scope of content

To perform this unit effectively you will need to know and understand the following:

Chapter

1 Use control accounts

1.1 Produce control accounts   2

Learners need to understand:

- 1.1.1 the purpose of the receivables and payables ledger control accounts (part of the double-entry bookkeeping system)
- 1.1.2 the purpose of the VAT control account.

Learners need to be able to:

- 1.1.3 prepare control accounts: - receivables ledger, payables ledger, VAT.
- 1.1.4 total and balance control accounts: balance carried down, balance brought down.

PRINCIPLES OF BOOKKEEPING CONTROLS

1.2 Reconcile control accounts   2

Learners need to understand:

- 1.2.1 reasons for reconciling the receivables and payables ledger control accounts with the receivables and payables ledgers.

Learners need to be able to:

- 1.2.2 total the balances of the individual receivables and payables ledger accounts:
  - receivables ledger debit/credit balances
  - payables ledger debit/credit balances
- 1.2.3 identify discrepancies between the receivables and payables ledger control accounts and the individual customer and supplier accounts
- 1.2.4 reconcile control accounts
  - receivables ledger
  - payables ledger
- 1.2.5 identify reasons for discrepancies between the receivables and payables ledger control accounts and the individual customer and supplier accounts.

2 Reconcile a bank statement with the cash book

2.1 Payment methods   5

Learners need to understand:

- 2.1.1 different payment methods:
  - cash
  - cheque
  - debit card
  - credit card
  - bank draft
  - standing order
  - direct debit
  - BACS (Bankers' Automated Clearing Services)
  - direct credit
  - CHAPS (Clearing House Automated Payment System)
  - Faster Payments

PRINCIPLES OF BOOKKEEPING CONTROLS

- 2.1.2 that different payment methods affect the bank balance in different ways:
  - reduce funds on the date of payment
  - reduce funds at a later date
  - have no effect.

2.2 Use the bank statement to update the cash book   5

Learners need to understand:

- 2.2.1 reasons for reconciling the bank statement with the cash book
- 2.2.2 the items that can cause differences between bank statements and the cash book:
  - opening balances
  - bank interest paid/received
  - bank charges
  - automated payments/receipts
  - timing differences:
    - outstanding lodgements
    - unpresented cheques.

Learners need to be able to:

- 2.2.3 update the cash book using the bank statement:
  - unrecorded
  - duplicated
- 2.2.4 total and balance the cash book:
  - credit/debit balance carried down
  - credit/debit balance brought down.

2.3 Complete bank reconciliation statements   5

Learners need to be able to:

- 2.3.1 complete bank reconciliation statements using:
  - closing bank statement balance
  - timing differences:
    - unpresented cheques
    - outstanding lodgements
  - closing cash book balance.

PRINCIPLES OF BOOKKEEPING CONTROLS

3 Use the journal

3.1 Produce journal entries to record bookkeeping transactions   1, 2, 4

Learners need to understand:

- 3.1.1 the purpose of the journal as a book of prime entry (manual and digital)
- 3.1.2 how the journal is used to record:
    - opening entries
    - irrecoverable debts written off
    - payroll transactions.

Learners need to be able to:

- 3.1.3 process journal entries to the general ledger accounts
- 3.1.4 record opening entries
- 3.1.5 record entries to write off irrecoverable debts:
    - record VAT where appropriate
    - calculate VAT from gross amounts
    - calculate VAT from net amounts
- 3.1.6 record entries for payroll transactions:
    - wages control account
    - gross pay
    - income tax
    - employer's and employees' National Insurance Contributions (NICs)
    - employer's and employees' pensions
    - voluntary deductions.

3.2 Produce journal entries to correct errors not disclosed by the trial balance   3

Learners need to understand:

- 3.2.1 the difference between errors disclosed and not disclosed by the trial balance

PRINCIPLES OF BOOKKEEPING CONTROLS

- 3.2.2 types of errors not disclosed by the trial balance (manual and digital):
  - error of commission
  - error of omission
  - error of original entry
  - error of principle
  - reversal of entries
  - compensating errors.

Learners need to be able to:

- 3.2.3 correct errors using the journal.

3.3 Produce journal entries to correct errors disclosed by the trial balance 3

Learners need to understand:

- 3.3.1 the purpose of a suspense account.

Learners need to be able to:

- 3.3.2 open a suspense account
- 3.3.3 correct errors and clear the suspense account using the journal.

4 Produce trial balances

4.1 Extract an initial trial balance 1

Learners need to know:

- 4.1.1 how to use the general ledger to extract balances
- 4.1.2 the column to use in the trial balance:
  - debit
  - credit.

Learners need to be able to:

- 4.1.3 transfer balances to the initial trial balance
- 4.1.4 total and balance the initial trial balance.

PRINCIPLES OF BOOKKEEPING CONTROLS

4.2 Redraft the trial balance following adjustments 1, 3

Learners need to be able to:

- 4.2.1 recalculate the balance of a general ledger account following journal entries
- 4.2.2 complete a trial balance from adjusted and unadjusted balances
- 4.2.3 balance the adjusted trial balance: total debit and credit columns.

Links with this unit

This unit links with:

- Level 2 Introduction to Bookkeeping
- Level 2 The Business Environment
- Level 3 Financial Accounting: Preparing Financial Statements
- Level 4 Cash and Financial Management

THE ASSESSMENT

Test specification for this unit assessment

Assessment type
Computer based assessment

Marking type
Computer marked

Duration of exam
1½ hours

The assessment for this unit consists of 8 compulsory, independent, tasks.

The competency level for AAT assessment is 70%.

Learning outcomes		Weighting
1	Use control accounts	25%
2	Reconcile a bank statement with the cash book	25%
3	Use the journal	25%
4	Produce trial balances	25%
Total		100%

APPRENTICESHIP LEARNERS ONLY

UNIT LINK TO THE END POINT ASSESSMENT (EPA)

To achieve the Accounts/Finance Assistant apprenticeship learners must pass the following assessments in the L2 Certificate in Accounting:

- Introduction to Bookkeeping
- Principles of Bookkeeping Controls
- Principles of Costing

There will also be a structured interview supported by a portfolio of evidence summary and an integrated knowledge test. The integrated qualification for AAT Level 2 Certificate in Accounting is:

- Business Environment

STUDY SKILLS

Preparing to study

Devise a study plan

Determine which times of the week you will study.

Split these times into sessions of at least one hour for study of new material. Any shorter periods could be used for revision or practice.

Put the times you plan to study onto a study plan for the weeks from now until the assessment and set yourself targets for each period of study – in your sessions make sure you cover the whole course, activities and the associated questions in the study text at the back of the manual.

If you are studying more than one unit at a time, try to vary your subjects as this can help to keep you interested and see subjects as part of wider knowledge.

When working through your course, compare your progress with your plan and, if necessary, re-think your work (perhaps including extra sessions) or, if you are ahead, do some extra revision / practice questions.

Effective studying

Active reading

You are not expected to learn the text by rote. You must understand what you are reading and be able to use it to pass the assessment and develop good practice.

A good technique is to use SQ3Rs – Survey, Question, Read, Recall, Review:

1. **Survey the chapter**

    Look at the headings and read the introduction, knowledge, skills and content, so as to get an overview of what the chapter deals with.

2. **Question**

    While surveying the chapter ask yourself the questions you hope the chapter will answer for you.

PRINCIPLES OF BOOKKEEPING CONTROLS

3 Read

Read through the chapter thoroughly working through the activities.

4 Recall

At the end of each section and at the end of the chapter, try to recall the main ideas of the section/chapter without referring to the text. This is best done after short break of a couple of minutes after the reading stage.

5 Review

Check that your recall notes are correct.

You may also find it helpful to re-read the chapter to try and see the topic(s) it deals with as a whole.

Note-taking

Taking notes is a useful way of learning, but do not simply copy out the text.

The notes must:

- be in your own words
- be concise
- cover the key points
- be well organised
- be modified as you study further chapters in this text or in related ones.

Trying to summarise a chapter without referring to the text can be a useful way of determining which areas you know and which you don't.

Three ways of taking notes

1 Summarise the key points of a chapter

2 Make linear notes

A list of headings, subdivided with sub-headings listing the key points.

If you use linear notes, you can use different colours to highlight key points and keep topic areas together.

Use plenty of space to make your notes easy to use.

3   Try a diagrammatic form

The most common of which is a mind map.

To make a mind map, put the main heading in the centre of the paper and put a circle around it.

Draw lines radiating from this to the main sub-headings which again have circles around them.

Continue the process from the sub-headings to sub-sub-headings.

Annotating the text

You may find it useful to underline or highlight key points in your study text – but do be selective.

You may also wish to make notes in the margins.

Revision phase

Kaplan has produced material specifically designed for your final assessment preparation for this unit.

These include pocket notes and an exam kit with questions specifically in the style of the new syllabus.

Further guidance on how to approach the final stage of your studies is given in these materials.

Further reading

In addition to this text, you should also read the 'Accounting Technician' magazine every month to keep abreast of any guidance from the examiners.

Double-entry bookkeeping

PRINCIPLES OF BOOKKEEPING CONTROLS

Introduction

A sound knowledge of double-entry bookkeeping underpins many of the learning outcomes and skills required for Principles of Bookkeeping Controls. Double-entry bookkeeping is essential knowledge in order to pass this unit and candidates will be assessed on it in the examination. Although much of the content of this chapter should be familiar from Introduction to Bookkeeping, it is essential that it is covered in order to build upon this basic knowledge.

ASSESSMENT CRITERIA

Produce journal entries to record bookkeeping transactions (3.1)

Extract an initial trial balance (4.1)

Redraft the trial balance following adjustments (4.2)

CONTENTS

1. Principles of double-entry bookkeeping
2. Overview of the accounting system
3. Rules of double-entry bookkeeping
4. Double-entry – cash transactions
5. Double-entry – credit transactions
6. Balancing a ledger account
7. Ledger accounting and the trial balance

1 Principles of double-entry bookkeeping

1.1 Introduction

Double-entry bookkeeping is based upon three basic principles:

- the dual effect principle
- the separate entity principle
- the accounting equation.

1.2 The dual effect

Definition – The dual effect principle

The principle of the dual effect is that **every** business transaction has **two** effects.

For example, if a business buys goods for cash then the two effects are:

- cash has decreased
- the business has purchased goods.

The principle of double-entry bookkeeping is that each of these effects must be shown in the ledger accounts by a **debit entry** in one account and an equal **credit entry** in another account.

Every transaction that a business undertakes has **two equal and opposite effects.**

1.3 The separate entity concept

Definition – The separate entity concept

The separate entity concept is that the business is a completely separate accounting entity from the owner.

Therefore if the owner pays personal money into a business bank account this money becomes the capital of the business, which is owed back to the owner. Similarly, if the owner takes money out of the business in the form of drawings, then the amount of capital owed to the owner is reduced.

The business itself is a completely separate entity from the owner of the business.

PRINCIPLES OF BOOKKEEPING CONTROLS

1.4 The accounting equation

At its simplest, the accounting equation says that:

Assets = Liabilities.

The owner's capital can be treated as a special form of liability, meaning the accounting equation is then:

Assets = Liabilities + Capital

Or, rearranged:

Assets – Liabilities = Capital.

Profit will increase the owner's capital and drawings will reduce it, so that the equation can be written as:

Assets – Liabilities = Capital + Profit – Drawings.

1.5 Definitions

Definition – Asset

An asset is a resource with economic value that is owned or controlled, with an expectation that it will provide a future benefit.

Assets are classified as either non-current assets or current assets. Assets may be tangible physical items or intangible items with no physical form.

Definition – Non-current assets

Non-current assets are assets that will be used within the business over a long period (usually greater than one year), e.g. land and buildings.

Definition – Current assets

Current assets are assets that are expected to be realised within the business in the normal course of trading (usually a period less than one year) e.g. inventory.

Double-entry bookkeeping: Chapter 1

 Definition – Liability

A liability is an obligation to transfer something of value (such as an asset) as a result of past transactions or events. For example, owing a balance to a credit supplier.

 Definition – Current liabilities

Current liabilities are the short-term payables of a business. Current liabilities are typically due to be paid within twelve months of the statement of financial position date e.g. trade payables.

 Definition – Non-current liabilities

Non-current liabilities are payables that will be paid over a longer period, typically in excess of one year of the statement of financial position date e.g. loans.

Test your understanding 1

Place the following account names under the correct headings.

Receivables
Bank overdraft
VAT payable
Motor van
Land

Inventory
Payables
Computers
Cash

Non-current assets	Current assets	Current liabilities

PRINCIPLES OF BOOKKEEPING CONTROLS

Definition – Capital/equity

Capital is the 'residual interest' in a business and represents what is left when the business is wound up, all the assets sold and all the outstanding liabilities paid. It is effectively what would be repaid to the owners if the business ceased to trade.

Definition – Income

Income is the recognition in profit of the inflow of economic benefit to the entity in the reporting period. For example, earning sales revenue.

Definition – Expense

Expense is the recognition of the outflow of economic benefit from an entity in the reporting period. For example, rent paid or electricity costs.

Test your understanding 2

Reeva Anderson is the owner of a business and notices an amount of £50,000 on the trial balance called 'Capital'. Reeva is unsure what this account represents.

Briefly explain what a capital account represents.

Test your understanding 3

Mandla starts in business with capital of £20,000, in the form of cash of £15,000 and non-current assets of £5,000.

In the first three days of trading, the following transactions occurred:

- Purchases £4,000 of inventory on credit terms. The supplier allows one month's credit.
- Sells inventory costing £1,500 for £2,000 and allows the customer a fortnight's credit.
- Purchases a motor vehicle for £6,000 and pays by bank transfer.

The accounting equation at the start would be:

Assets less liabilities = Capital
£20,000 – £0 = £20,000

Required:

Update the accounting equation after all the transactions had taken place.

2 Overview of the accounting system

2.1 Overview of the accounting system

A business may enter into a large number of transactions on a daily basis. Keeping track of all these transactions can be a difficult process.

To ensure that a business manages to keep a record of all sales, purchases and expenses incurred, and the assets, liabilities and capital held at any point, the transactions are recorded in an accounting system.

1. Business transaction
2. Business document
3. Books of prime entry
4. Ledger accounts
5. Trial balance

1   Initially a **business transaction** will take place: a credit sale, a credit purchase, a cash sale, a cash purchase, another expense either paid from the bank or by cash, cash paid into the bank, withdrawal of cash from the bank and owner's drawings.

2   A **business document** will be produced e.g. an invoice.

PRINCIPLES OF BOOKKEEPING CONTROLS

3   The transaction and details from the business document will be entered into the **books of prime entry**. A book of prime entry is where a transaction is first recorded. There are several books of prime entry, which may also be referred to as 'day books'.

4   The totals in the books of prime entry are transferred into **ledger accounts** as part of the **general ledger** on a regular basis. Ledger accounts are used as part of the double-entry accounting system.

5   A **trial balance** is a list of all of the ledger accounts in the accounting system. The total of debits should equal the total of credits within a trial balance. The trial balance can be used as a control to check that transactions have been recorded correctly in the double-entry system prior to the preparation of the financial statements.

2.2 Books of prime entry

A book of prime entry is the place where the transaction (which is detailed on a business document) is first recorded in the books of the business. Books of prime entry may also be referred to as day books. There are several day books, which will be briefly reviewed in this chapter:

 Definition – Sales day book

The sales day book is a list of the credit sales invoices that are to be processed for a given period (e.g. a week).

Definition – Sales returns day book

The sales returns day book is a list of the credit notes that are to be processed for a given period.

Definition – Purchases day book

The purchases day book is a list of the credit purchase invoices that are to be processed for a given period.

Definition – Purchases returns day book

The purchases returns day book is a list of the credit notes that have been received from suppliers for a given period.

Definition – Cash book

A cash book is a record of cash receipts and payments for a given period. It can form part of the double-entry bookkeeping system as well as being a book of prime entry.

Definition – Discounts allowed day book

The discounts allowed day book is used to record prompt payment discounts given to credit customers. These discounts have not been deducted at the point of the credit sale being recorded within the sales day book as they were offered on a conditional basis.

Definition – Discounts received day book

The discounts received day book is used to record prompt payment discounts received from credit suppliers. These discounts have not been deducted at the point of the credit purchase being recorded in the purchases day book as they were offered on a conditional basis.

PRINCIPLES OF BOOKKEEPING CONTROLS

Definition – Petty cash book

A petty cash book is used to record all petty cash receipts and payments.

2.3 The general ledger

Definition – General ledger

A general ledger contains all the ledger accounts for recording transactions occurring within an entity.

Note: AAT's preferred term is 'general ledger' but the general ledger may also be referred to as the 'main' or 'nominal' ledger.

2.4 The subsidiary ledger

Definition – Subsidiary ledger

A subsidiary ledger provides specific details of individual customer and supplier balances contained within the general ledger receivables and payables balances.

Definition – Subsidiary receivables ledger

A subsidiary receivables ledger is more commonly referred to as the 'receivables ledger'. It is a set of receivable balances owed from individual customers.

Definition – Subsidiary payables ledger

A subsidiary payables ledger is more commonly referred to as the 'payables ledger'. It is a set of payable balances owed to individual suppliers.

3 Rules of double-entry bookkeeping

3.1 Double-entry bookkeeping rules

There are a number of rules that can help to determine which two accounts are to be debited and credited for a transaction:

- When money is paid out by a business, this is a credit entry in the cash or bank account.
- When money is received by a business, this is a debit entry in the cash or bank account.
- An increase in an asset is always recorded on the debit side of the asset's account.
- An increase in a liability is always recorded on the credit side of the liabilities account.
- An expense is recorded as a debit entry in the expense account.
- Income is recorded as a credit entry in the income account.

3.2 The golden rule

Every debit has an equal and opposite credit.

Ledger account	
A debit entry represents	**A credit entry represents**
An increase to an asset	An increase to a liability
A decrease to a liability	A decrease to an asset
An item of expense	An item of income

For increases, remember this as DEAD CLIC

Ledger account	
Debits increase:	**Credits increase:**
Expenses	Liabilities
Assets	Income
Drawings	Capital

PRINCIPLES OF BOOKKEEPING CONTROLS

3.3 Opening balances

The balance on an account at the start of a period is known as an opening balance.

A task in the assessment may involve the creation of opening balances. The key will be to identify whether the opening balance should be shown as a debit or a credit.

The mnemonic DEAD/CLIC will help determine if an entry should be made on the debit side or on the credit side of a ledger account.

Ledger account	
Debit:	**Credit:**
• **E**xpenses	• **L**iabilities
• **A**ssets	• **I**ncome
• **D**rawings	• **C**apital

Example 1

You are told that the opening balance on the receivables ledger control account is £33,600, the opening balance on the purchases account is £115,200 and the opening balance on the payables ledger control account is £12,700.

You are required to enter these into the relevant ledger accounts.

Solution

Receivables ledger control account

	£		£
Balance brought down	33,600		

Purchases account

	£		£
Balance brought down	115,200		

Payables ledger control account

	£		£
		Balance brought down	12,700

Assets and expenses normally have opening debit balances. Liabilities and income normally have opening credit balances.

KAPLAN PUBLISHING

3.4 Journals

A journal entry is a written instruction to the bookkeeper to enter a double-entry into the general ledger accounts.

A journal can simply be the debit and credit that are required, but can include a description underneath to explain the journal.

The journal will be considered further in later chapters, but an example of the journal needed to record opening balances is shown below.

Example 2

Record the journal entries needed in the general ledger to account for the following balances.

Receivables ledger control account	33,600
Purchases	115,200
Payables ledger control account	12,700
Sales	138,240
Rent and rates	2,140

Solution

Receivables ledger control account	33,600	Debit
Purchases	115,200	Debit
Payables ledger control account	12,700	Credit
Sales	138,240	Credit
Rent and rates	2,140	Debit

To record the opening balances.

PRINCIPLES OF BOOKKEEPING CONTROLS

 Test your understanding 4

The following are the opening balances for a new business. Complete the journal to record these balances.

Account name	Amount £	Debit/Credit
Bank overdraft	6,975	
Cash	275	
VAT payable	2,390	
Motor vehicles	10,500	
Plant and machinery	25,700	
Loan from bank	12,000	
Capital	20,020	
Motor expenses	1,540	
Rent and rates	2,645	
Miscellaneous expenses	725	

4 Double entry – cash transactions

4.1 Introduction

Introduction to Bookkeeping first covered double-entry bookkeeping concepts. Let us revise some double-entry bookkeeping techniques using the accounting for cash transactions – remember that money paid out is a credit entry and money received is a debit entry in the cash account.

Cash/Bank account	
DEBIT	**CREDIT**
Money in	Money out

Example 3

Dani Bianchi decides to set up in business as a sole trader by paying £20,000 into a business bank account. The following transactions then occur:

(i) the purchase of a delivery van for £5,500 paid through the bank

(ii) a purchase of goods for resale by debit card for £2,000

(iii) payment of £500 shop rental in cash

(iv) sale of goods for cash of £2,500

(v) Dani took £200 of cash for personal expenses.

Note that cash received or paid is normally deemed to pass through the bank account.

State the two effects of each of these transactions and record them in the relevant ledger accounts.

Solution

Money paid into the business bank account by Dani:

- increase in cash
- capital now owed back to Dani.

Double entry:

- a debit to the bank account as money is coming in
- a credit to the capital account.

Bank account

	£		£
Capital	20,000		

Capital account

	£		£
		Bank	20,000

(i) The purchase of a delivery van for £5,500 paid through the bank

- cash decreases
- the business has a non-current asset, the van.

PRINCIPLES OF BOOKKEEPING CONTROLS

Double entry:

- credit to the bank account as cash is being paid out
- debit to an asset account, the van account.

Bank account

	£		£
Capital	20,000	Van	5,500

Van account

	£		£
Bank	5,500		

(ii) A purchase of goods for resale by debit card for £2,000

- decrease in cash
- increase in purchases.

Double entry:

- credit to the bank account as money is paid out
- debit to the purchases account, an expense account.

Purchases of inventory are always recorded in a purchases account and never in an inventory account.

Bank account

	£		£
Capital	20,000	Van	5,500
		Purchases	2,000

Purchases account

	£		£
Bank	2,000		

(iii) Payment of £500 shop rental in cash

- decrease in cash
- expense incurred.

Double entry:

- credit to the bank account as money is paid out
- debit to the rent account, an expense.

Bank account

	£		£
Capital	20,000	Van	5,500
		Purchases	2,000
		Rent	500

Rent account

	£		£
Bank	500		

(iv) Sale of goods for cash of £2,500

- cash increases
- sales increase.

Double entry:

- debit to the bank account as money is coming in
- credit to the sales account, being income.

Bank account

	£		£
Capital	20,000	Van	5,500
Sales	2,500	Purchases	2,000
		Rent	500

Sales account

	£		£
		Bank	2,500

(v) Dani took £200 of cash for own personal expenses

- cash decreases
- drawings increase (money taken out of the business by the owner).

Double entry:

- credit to the bank account as money is paid out
- debit to the drawings account.

PRINCIPLES OF BOOKKEEPING CONTROLS

Bank account			
	£		£
Capital	20,000	Van	5,500
Sales	2,500	Purchases	2,000
		Rent	500
		Drawings	200

Drawings account			
	£		£
Bank	200		

5 Double entry – credit transactions

5.1 Introduction

Let's now revise sales and purchases on credit. For sales and purchases on credit there is no cash increase or decrease. Remember that an increase in income is a credit entry and an increase in an expense is a debit entry.

Example 4

Dani now makes some further transactions:

(i) purchases are made on credit for £3,000
(ii) sales are made on credit for £4,000
(iii) Dani pays £2,000 to the credit suppliers
(iv) £2,500 is received from the credit customers
(v) Dani returned goods costing £150 to a supplier
(vi) goods which had cost £200 were returned by a customer.

State the two effects of each of these transactions and write them up in the appropriate ledger accounts.

Solution

(i) Purchases are made on credit for £3,000

- increase in purchases
- increase in payables (PLCA).

Double entry:

- debit entry to the purchases account, an expense
- credit to the payables account, a liability.

Purchases account

	£		£
Bank	2,000		
Payables	3,000		

Payables account (PLCA)

	£		£
		Purchases	3,000

(ii) Sales are made on credit for £4,000

- increase in sales
- increase in receivables.

Double entry:

- credit entry to the sales account, income
- debit entry to the receivables account, an asset.

Sales account

	£		£
		Bank	2,500
		Receivables	4,000

Receivables account (SLCA)

	£		£
Sales	4,000		

(iii) Dani pays £2,000 to the suppliers

- decrease in cash
- decrease in payables.

Double entry:

- credit entry to the bank account as money is paid out
- debit entry to payables as the liability is reduced.

Bank account

	£		£
Capital	20,000	Van	5,500
Sales	2,500	Purchases	2,000
		Rent	500
		Drawings	200
		Payables	2,000

Payables account (PLCA)

	£		£
Bank	2,000	Purchases	3,000

(iv) £2,500 is received from the credit customers

- increase in cash
- decrease in receivables.

Double entry:

- debit entry in the bank account as money is received
- credit entry to reduce receivables.

Bank account

	£		£
Capital	20,000	Van	5,500
Sales	2,500	Purchases	2,000
Receivables	2,500	Rent	500
		Drawings	200
		Payables	2,000

Receivables account (SLCA)

	£		£
Sales	4,000	Bank	2,500

(v) Dani returned goods costing £150 to a supplier
- purchases returns increase
- payables decrease.

Double entry:
- debit entry to decrease the payables account
- credit entry to the purchases returns account (because this is the opposite of purchases which are a debit entry).

Payables account (PLCA)

	£		£
Bank	2,000	Purchases	3,000
Purchases returns	150		

Purchases returns account

	£		£
		Payables	150

(vi) Goods were returned by a customer which had cost £200
- sales returns increase
- receivables decrease.

Double entry:
- credit entry to decrease the receivables account
- debit entry to sales returns (the opposite to sales which is a credit entry).

Receivables account (SLCA)

	£		£
Sales	4,000	Bank	2,500
		Sales returns	200

Sales returns account

	£		£
Receivables	200		

PRINCIPLES OF BOOKKEEPING CONTROLS

6 Balancing a ledger account

6.1 Introduction

Once the transactions for a period have been recorded in the ledger accounts it is likely that the owner will want to know certain matters, such as how much cash there is in the bank account, or how much has been spent on purchases? This can be found by balancing the ledger accounts.

6.2 Procedure for balancing a ledger account

The following steps should be followed when balancing a ledger account:

Step 1

Total both the debit and credit columns to find the higher total – enter this figure as the total for both the debit and credit columns.

Step 2

For the side that does not add up to this total, put in the balancing figure and call it the balance carried down, or 'bal c/d.'

Step 3

Enter the bal c/d (from step 2) on the opposite side of the T account but below the totals and describe it as the balance brought down ('bal b/d'). .

Example 5

Now balance Dani's bank account

Bank account

	£		£
Capital	20,000	Van	5,500
Sales	2,500	Purchases	2,000
Receivables	2,500	Rent	500
		Drawings	200
		Payables	2,000

Double-entry bookkeeping: Chapter 1

	Bank account		
	£		£
Capital	20,000	Van	5,500
Sales	2,500	Purchases	2,000
Receivables	2,500	Rent	500
		Drawings	200
		Payables	2,000
		Balance c/d **Step 2**	14,800
Step 1	25,000	**Step 1**	25,000
Balance b/d **Step 3**	14,800		

 Test your understanding 5

Dave

Dave had the following transactions during January 20X3:

1. Introduced £500 cash as capital.
2. Purchased goods on credit from A Ltd worth £200.
3. Paid rent for one month of £20.
4. Paid electricity for one month of £50.
5. Purchased a car for £100 cash.
6. Sold half of the goods on credit to X Ltd for £175.
7. Drew £30 for own expenses.
8. Sold the remainder of the goods for £210 cash.

Required:

Write up the relevant ledger accounts necessary to record the above transactions and balance off the accounts.

Test your understanding 6

(a) Show by means of ledger accounts how the following transactions would be recorded in the books of Bertie Dooks, a seller of second-hand books:

(i) paid in cash £5,000 as capital

(ii) took the lease of a stall and paid six months' rent – the yearly rental was £300

(iii) spent £140 cash on the purchase of books from W Smith

(iv) purchased books on credit from J Fox at a cost of £275

(v) paid an odd-job professional £25 to paint the exterior of the stall and repair a broken lock

(vi) put an advertisement in the local paper at a cost of £2

(vii) sold three volumes containing The Complete Works of William Shakespeare for £35 cash

(viii) sold a similar set on credit to a local school for £3

(ix) paid J Fox £175 for the amount due

(x) received £1 from the school

(xi) purchased cleaning materials at a cost of £2 and paid £3 to a cleaner

(xii) took £5 from the business for personal expenses.

(b) Balance off the ledgers, clearly showing balance carried down (c/d) and balance brought down (b/d).

Double-entry bookkeeping: **Chapter 1**

7 Ledger accounting and the trial balance

7.1 Introduction

 Definition – Trial balance

A trial balance is the list of the balances on all of the ledger accounts in an organisation's general (aka main or nominal) ledger.

7.2 Trial balance

A trial balance lists all of the ledger account balances in the general ledger. The trial balance will appear as a list of debit balances and credit balances. If the double entry has been correctly carried out, the debit balance total should be equal to the credit balance total.

7.3 Preparing the trial balance

When all of the entries have been made in the ledger accounts for a period, the trial balance will then be prepared.

Step 1

Balance off each ledger account and bring down the closing balance.

Step 2

List each balance brought down as either a debit balance or a credit balance.

Step 3

Total the debit balances and the credit balances to see if they are equal.

PRINCIPLES OF BOOKKEEPING CONTROLS

 Example 6

Given below are the initial transactions for Sakash, a sole trader. Enter the transactions in the ledger accounts using a separate account for each receivable and payable. Produce the trial balance for Sakash at the end of 12 January 20X1.

On 1 Jan	Sakash put £12,500 into the business bank account.
On 2 Jan	Sakash bought goods for resale costing £750 on credit from J Oliver. Sakash also bought £1,000 of goods on credit from K Hardy.
On 3 Jan	Sold goods for £800 to E Morecombe on credit.
On 5 Jan	Sakash returned £250 worth of goods bought from J Oliver, being substandard goods.
On 6 Jan	Sold goods on credit to A Wise for £1,000.
On 7 Jan	Sakash withdrew £100 from the bank for personal use.
On 8 Jan	Bought a further £1,500 worth of goods from K Hardy, again on credit.
On 9 Jan	A Wise returned £200 worth of goods.
On 10 Jan	The business paid J Oliver £500 via the bank, and K Hardy £1,000 also via the bank.
On 12 Jan	Sakash banked a cheque for £800 received from E Morecombe.

Solution

Step 1

Enter the transactions into the ledger accounts and then balance off each ledger account. Use a separate ledger account for each receivable and payable. (Note that in most examinations you will be required to complete the double entry for receivables and payables in the receivables and payables ledger control accounts, but for practice here we are using separate accounts for each customer and supplier).

Step 2

Balance off each of the ledger accounts.

Capital account

	£			£
		1 Jan	Bank	12,500

Sales account

		£			£
	Balance c/d	1,800	3 Jan	E Morecombe	800
			6 Jan	A Wise	1,000
		1,800			1,800
				Balance b/d	1,800

Purchases account

		£			£
2 Jan	J Oliver	750			
2 Jan	K Hardy	1,000			
8 Jan	K Hardy	1,500		Balance c/d	3,250
		3,250			3,250
	Balance b/d	3,250			

Purchases returns account

		£			£
			5 Jan	J Oliver	250

Sales returns account

		£			£
9 Jan	A Wise	200			

Drawings account

		£			£
7 Jan	Bank	100			

Bank account

		£			£
1 Jan	Capital	12,500	7 Jan	Drawings	100
12 Jan	E Morecombe	800	10 Jan	J Oliver	500
				K Hardy	1,000
				Balance c/d	11,700
		13,300			13,300
	Balance b/d	11,700			

PRINCIPLES OF BOOKKEEPING CONTROLS

E Morecombe account

		£			£
3 Jan	Sales	800	12 Jan	Bank	800

A Wise account

		£			£
6 Jan	Sales	1,000	9 Jan	Sales returns	200
				Balance c/d	800
		1,000			1,000
	Balance b/d	800			

J Oliver account

		£			£
5 Jan	Purchases returns	250	2 Jan	Purchases	750
10 Jan	Bank	500			
		750			750

K Hardy account

		£			£
10 Jan	Bank	1,000	2 Jan	Purchases	1,000
	Balance c/d	1,500	8 Jan	Purchases	1,500
		2,500			2,500
				Balance b/d	1,500

Note that accounts with only one entry do not need to be balanced, as this entry is the final balance on the account.

Step 3

Produce the trial balance by listing each balance brought down as either a debit balance or a credit balance.

Make sure to use the balance brought down below the total line as the balance to list in the trial balance.

Step 4

Total the debit and credit columns to check that they are equal.

> **Trial balance as at 12 January 20X1**
>
> | | Debits £ | Credits £ |
> |---|---:|---:|
> | Capital | | 12,500 |
> | Sales | | 1,800 |
> | Purchases | 3,250 | |
> | Purchases returns | | 250 |
> | Sales returns | 200 | |
> | Drawings | 100 | |
> | Bank | 11,700 | |
> | A Wise | 800 | |
> | K Hardy | | 1,500 |
> | | 16,050 | 16,050 |
>
> **Note:** E Morecombe and J Oliver have a nil balance so have not appeared in the trial balance.

7.4 Initial and adjusted trial balances

It is important to distinguish between an initial trial balance and an adjusted trial balance.

An **initial trial balance** provides an initial summary of the general ledger accounts prior to entering any adjusting entries. One of the main purposes of a trial balance is to serve as a check on the double entry. If the trial balance does not balance, i.e. the debit and credit totals are not equal, then some errors have been made in the double entry (this will be covered in more detail in a later chapter).

An **adjusted trial balance** is prepared after all the adjusting entries have been posted into the appropriate general ledger accounts. The adjusted trial balance is completed to ensure that the financial statements will be accurate and in balance.

The trial balances described above can also serve as the basis for preparing another version of the TB called 'the extended trial balance' which feeds directly into the financial statements of the organisation. The extended trial balance and preparation of financial statements is considered later in your studies and is not part of this unit.

PRINCIPLES OF BOOKKEEPING CONTROLS

7.5 Debit or credit balance?

After balancing a ledger account, it should be easy to see which side, debit or credit, the balance brought down is on. However if given a list of balances rather than the ledger accounts, then it can be more difficult to decide which side the balance should be shown in the trial balance.

There are some rules to help here:

- assets are debit balances
- expenses are debit balances
- liabilities are credit balances
- income is a credit balance.

This can be remembered using the 'DEAD CLIC' mnemonic.

7.6 An adjusted trial balance

As discussed previously, an adjusted trial balance is prepared to show updated balances after any adjusting entries have been made. It is prepared by creating a number of journal entries, designed to account for any transactions that have not yet been completed.

These transactions may include, for example, payroll expenses or the correction of errors, which we will be covering later in Principles of Bookkeeping Controls.

Double-entry bookkeeping: Chapter 1

Test your understanding 7

1   The bank account for January is as follows:

Bank account

	£		£
Balance b/d	1,900	Payables	7,000
Receivables	2,500		
Cash sales	500		

At the end of the month there is a **debit/credit** balance of **£7,000/£4,900/£2,100.**

Circle the correct answer

2   'To increase a liability a debit entry is made.'
    True or false?
            True
            False
    Tick the correct answer for task 2

    Circle the correct answer for task 3, 4, 5, 6 and 7

3   When a sole trader uses goods for resale for their own personal use, the drawings account is **debited / credited** and the purchases account is **debited / credited**.

4   When a supplier is paid, the bank account is **debited / credited** and the supplier's payable account is **debited / credited**.

5   When goods are sold to a receivable, the sales account is **debited / credited** and the receivable account is **debited / credited**.

6   A bank overdraft is a **debit / credit** account in the trial balance.

7   Discounts received are a **debit / credit** balance in the trial balance.

PRINCIPLES OF BOOKKEEPING CONTROLS

Test your understanding 8

The following balances have been extracted from the books of Freida at 31 December 20X2:

Prepare a trial balance at 31 December 20X2.

	£	Debit	Credit
Capital on 1 January 20X2	106,149		
Freehold factory at cost	360,000		
Motor vehicles at cost	126,000		
Inventories at 1 January 20X2	37,500		
Receivables	15,600		
Cash in hand	225		
Bank overdraft	82,386		
Payables	78,900		
Sales	318,000		
Purchases	165,000		
Rent and rates	35,400		
Discounts allowed	6,600		
Insurance	2,850		
Sales returns	10,500		
Purchase returns	6,300		
Loan from bank	240,000		
Sundry expenses	45,960		
Drawings	26,100		
TOTALS			

Test your understanding 9

Peter

From the following list of balances, to draw up a trial balance for Peter at 31 December 20X8:

	£
Fixtures and fittings	6,430
Delivery vans	5,790
Cash at bank (in funds)	3,720
General expenses	1,450
Receivables	2,760
Payables	3,250
Purchases	10,670
Sales revenue	25,340
Wages	4,550
Drawings	5,000
Lighting and heating	1,250
Rent, rates and insurance	2,070
Capital	15,100

Test your understanding 10

Lara

The following transactions took place in July 20X6:

1 July	Lara started a business selling cricket boots and put £200 in the bank.
2 July	Marlar lent Lara £1,000.
3 July	Bought goods from Greig Ltd on credit for £296.
4 July	Bought a motor van for £250 cash.
7 July	Made cash sales amounting to £105.
8 July	Paid motor expenses of £15.
9 July	Paid wages of £18.
10 July	Bought goods on credit from Knott Ltd for £85.
14 July	Paid insurance premium of £22.
25 July	Received £15 commission as a result of successful sales promotion of MCC cricket boots.
31 July	Paid an electricity bill of £17.

Required:

(a) Write up the ledger accounts in the books of Lara.

(b) Extract a trial balance at 31 July 20X6.

Test your understanding 11

Enter the following transactions for the month of May 20X6 into the appropriate ledger accounts and extract a trial balance as at 1 June 20X6.

Open a separate ledger account for each receivable and payable, and keep separate 'cash' and 'bank' ledger accounts. Balance off each account and prepare a trial balance.

20X6

1 May	Started in business by paying £6,800 into the bank.
3 May	Bought goods on credit from the following: J Johnson £400, D Nixon £300 and J Agnew £250.
5 May	Cash sales £300.
6 May	Paid rates by debit card of £100.
8 May	Paid wages of £50 in cash.
9 May	Sold goods on credit: K Homes £300, J Homes £300, B Hood £100.
10 May	Bought goods on credit: J Johnson £800, D Nixon £700.
11 May	Returned £150 goods to J Johnson.
15 May	Bought office fixtures for £600 by debit card.
18 May	Bought a motor vehicle for £3,500 and paid via bank transfer.
22 May	£100 of goods returned by J Homes.
25 May	Paid J Johnson £1,000, D Nixon £500, both by BACS.
26 May	Paid wages £150 by BACS.

PRINCIPLES OF BOOKKEEPING CONTROLS

 Test your understanding 12

Peter Wall

Peter Wall started business on 1 January 20X8 printing and selling astrology books. Peter introduced £10,000 capital and was given a loan of £10,000 by Oswald. The following is a list of transactions for the three months to 31 March 20X8:

1 Purchased printing equipment for £7,000 cash.
2 Purchased a delivery van for £400 on credit from Arnold.
3 Bought paper for £100 on credit from Butcher.
4 Bought ink for £10 cash.
5 Paid £25 for one quarter's rent and rates to 31 March 20X8.
6 Paid £40 for one year's insurance premium.
7 Sold £200 of books for cash and £100 on credit to Constantine.
8 Paid Oswald £450 representing the following:
   (i) Part repayment of principal.
   (ii) Interest calculated at an annual rate of 2% per annum for three months.
9 Received £60 from Constantine.
10 Paid £200 towards the delivery van and £50 towards the paper.
11 Having forgotten a part payment for the paper, Peter then paid Butcher a further £100.

Required:

(a) Write up all necessary ledger accounts, including cash.
(b) Extract a trial balance at 31 March 20X8 (before period-end accruals).

8 Summary

In this opening chapter, the basic principles of double-entry bookkeeping have been revised from your basic accounting studies.

The basic principles of double entry are of great importance for this unit and all students should be able to determine whether a particular balance on an account is a debit or a credit balance in the trial balance.

Test your understanding answers

Test your understanding 1

Non-current assets	Current assets	Current liabilities
Land	Inventory	Bank overdraft
Motor van	Receivables	VAT payable
Computers	Cash	Payables

Test your understanding 2

The balance on the capital account represents the investment made in the business by the owner. It is a special liability of the business, showing the amount payable to the owner at the statement of financial position date.

Test your understanding 3

Assets		
	Non-current assets (5,000 + 6,000)	11,000
	Cash (15,000 – 6,000)	9,000
	Inventory (4,000 – 1,500)	2,500
	Receivables	2,000
		24,500

Assets – Liabilities = Capital

£24,500 – £4,000 = £20,500

Capital has increased by the profit made on the sale of inventory.

Double-entry bookkeeping: Chapter 1

Test your understanding 4

Account name	Amount £	Debit/Credit
Bank overdraft	6,975	Credit
Cash	275	Debit
VAT payable	2,390	Credit
Motor vehicles	10,500	Debit
Plant and machinery	25,700	Debit
Loan from bank	12,000	Credit
Capital	20,020	Credit
Motor expenses	1,540	Debit
Rent and rates	2,645	Debit
Miscellaneous expenses	725	Debit

Test your understanding 5

Dave

Cash

	£		£
Capital	500	Rent	20
Revenue	210	Electricity	50
		Drawings	30
		Car	100
		Balance c/d	510
	710		710
Balance b/d	510		

Capital

	£		£
Balance c/d	500	Cash	500
	500		500
		Balance b/d	500

PRINCIPLES OF BOOKKEEPING CONTROLS

Purchases

	£		£
Payables (A Ltd)	200	Balance c/d	200
	200		200
Balance b/d	200		

Payables

	£		£
Balance c/d	200	Purchases	200
	200		200
		Balance b/d	200

Revenue

	£		£
Balance c/d	385	Receivables (X Ltd)	175
		Cash	210
	385		385
		Balance b/d	385

Receivables

	£		£
Revenue	175	Balance c/d	175
	175		175
Balance b/d	175		

Electricity

	£		£
Cash	50	Balance c/d	50
	50		50
Balance b/d	50		

Rent

	£		£
Cash	20	Balance c/d	20
	20		20
Balance b/d	20		

Motor car

	£		£
Cash	100	Balance c/d	100
	100		100
Balance b/d	100		

Drawings

	£		£
Cash	30	Balance c/d	30
	30		30
Balance b/d	30		

Test your understanding 6

Ledger accounts

Cash account

	£		£
Capital account (i)	5,000	Rent (six months) (ii)	150
Sales (vii)	35	Purchases (iii)	140
Receivables (x)	1	Repairs (v)	25
		Advertising (vi)	2
		Payables (ix)	175
		Cleaning (xi)	5
		Drawings (xii)	5
		Balance c/d	4,534
	5,036		5,036
Balance b/d	4,534		

Payable account (J Fox)

	£		£
Cash (ix)	175	Purchases (iv)	275
Balance c/d	100		
	275		275
		Balance b/d	100

Receivable account (School)

	£		£
Sales (viii)	3	Cash (x)	1
		Balance c/d	2
	3		3
Balance b/d	2		

Capital account

	£		£
Balance c/d	5,000	Cash (i)	5,000
	5,000		5,000
		Balance b/d	5,000

Sales account

	£		£
		Cash (vii)	35
Balance c/d	38	Receivables (School) (viii)	3
	38		38
		Balance b/d	38

Purchases account

	£		£
Cash (iii)	140	Balance c/d	415
Payable (J Fox) (iv)	275		
	415		415
Balance b/d	415		

Rent account

	£		£
Cash (ii)	150	Balance c/d	150
	150		150
Balance b/d	150		

Repairs account

	£		£
Cash (v)	25	Balance c/d	25
	25		25
Balance b/d	25		

Advertising account

	£		£
Cash (vi)	2	Balance c/d	2
	2		2
Balance b/d	2		

Cleaning account

	£		£
Cash (xi)	5	Balance c/d	5
	5		5
Balance b/d	5		

Drawings account

	£		£
Cash (xii)	5	Balance c/d	5
	5		5
Balance b/d	5		

PRINCIPLES OF BOOKKEEPING CONTROLS

Test your understanding 7

1. The bank account for January is as follows:

Bank account

	£		£
Balance b/d	1,900	Payables	7,000
Receivables	2,500		
Cash sales	500		
Balance c/d	**2,100**		
	7,000		7,000
		Balance b/d	2,100

The correct answer is **CREDIT** of **£2,100**.

2. False.

3. When a sole trader uses goods for resale for their own personal use the drawings account is **debited** and the purchases account is **credited**.

4. When a supplier is paid the bank account is **credited** and the supplier's payable account is **debited**.

5. When goods are sold to a receivable, the sales account is **credited** and the receivable account is **debited**.

6. A bank overdraft is a **credit** balance in the trial balance.

7. Discounts received are a **credit** balance in the trial balance.

Test your understanding 8

Trial balance at 31 December 20X2

	Dr £	Cr £
Capital on 1 January 20X2		106,149
Freehold factory at cost	360,000	
Motor vehicles at cost	126,000	
Inventories at 1 January 20X2	37,500	
Receivables	15,600	
Cash in hand	225	
Bank overdraft		82,386
Payables		78,900
Sales		318,000
Purchases	165,000	
Rent and rates	35,400	
Discounts allowed	6,600	
Insurance	2,850	
Sales returns	10,500	
Purchase returns		6,300
Loan from bank		240,000
Sundry expenses	45,960	
Drawings	26,100	
	831,735	831,735

Test your understanding 9

Peter
Trial balance at 31 December 20X8

	£	£
Fixtures and fittings	6,430	
Delivery vans	5,790	
Cash at bank	3,720	
General expenses	1,450	
Receivables	2,760	
Payables		3,250
Purchases	10,670	
Revenue		25,340
Wages	4,550	
Drawings	5,000	
Lighting and heating	1,250	
Rent, rates and insurance	2,070	
Capital		15,100
	43,690	43,690

Test your understanding 10

Lara

(a)

Cash

	£		£
Capital	200	Motor van	250
Marlar – loan account	1,000	Motor expenses	15
Revenue	105	Wages	18
Commission	15	Insurance	22
		Electricity	17
		Balance c/d	998
	1,320		1,320
Balance b/d	998		

Purchases

	£		£
Payables	296	Balance c/d	381
Payables	85		
	381		381
Balance b/d	381		

Capital

	£		£
Balance c/d	200	Cash book	200
	200		200
		Balance b/d	200

Marlar – loan

	£		£
Balance c/d	1,000	Cash book	1,000
	1,000		1,000
		Balance b/d	1,000

Motor van

	£		£
Cash book	250	Balance c/d	250
	250		250
Balance b/d	250		

Sales revenue

	£		£
Balance c/d	105	Cash book	105
	105		105
		Balance b/d	105

Motor expenses

	£		£
Cash book	15	Balance c/d	15
	15		15
Balance b/d	15		

Wages

	£		£
Cash book	18	Balance c/d	18
	18		18
Balance b/d	18		

Insurance

	£		£
Cash book	22	Balance c/d	22
	22		22
Balance b/d	22		

Commission received			
	£		£
Balance c/d	15	Cash book	15
	15		15
		Balance b/d	15

Electricity			
	£		£
Cash book	17	Balance c/d	17
	17		17
Balance b/d	17		

Payables			
	£		£
Balance c/d	381	Purchases	296
		Purchases	85
	381		381
		Balance b/d	381

(b)

Lara

Trial balance at 31 July 20X6

	£	£
Cash	998	
Purchases	381	
Capital		200
Loan		1,000
Motor van	250	
Sales revenue		105
Motor expenses	15	
Wages	18	
Insurance	22	
Commission received		15
Electricity	17	
Payables		381
	1,701	1,701

Test your understanding 11

Cash account

	£		£
5 May Sales	300	8 May Wages	50
		31 May Balance c/d	250
	300		300
1 June Balance b/d	250		

Bank account

	£		£
1 May Capital	6,800	6 May Rates	100
		15 May Office fixtures	600
		18 May Motor vehicle	3,500
		25 May J Johnson	1,000
		D Nixon	500
		26 May Wages	150
		31 May Balance c/d	950
	6,800		6,800
1 June Balance b/d	950		

J Johnson account

	£		£
11 May Purchase returns	150	3 May Purchases	400
25 May Bank	1,000	10 May Purchases	800
31 May Balance c/d	50		
	1,200		1,200
		1 June Balance b/d	50

D Nixon account

	£		£
25 May Bank	500	3 May Purchases	300
31 May Balance c/d	500	10 May Purchases	700
	1,000		1,000
		1 June Balance b/d	500

J Agnew account

	£		£
31 May Balance c/d	250	3 May Purchases	250
		1 June Balance b/d	250

K Homes account

	£		£
9 May Sales	300	31 May Balance c/d	300
	300		300
1 June Balance b/d	300		

J Homes account

	£		£
9 May Sales	300	22 May Sales returns	100
		31 May Balance c/d	200
	300		300
1 June Balance b/d	200		

B Hood account

	£		£
9 May Sales	100	31 May Balance c/d	100
1 June Balance b/d	100		

Capital account

	£		£
31 May Balance c/d	6,800	1 May Bank	6,800
		1 June Balance b/d	6,800

Purchases account

		£		£
3 May	J Johnson	400		
	D Nixon	300		
	J Agnew	250		
10 May	J Johnson	800		
	D Nixon	700	31 May Balance c/d	2,450
		2,450		2,450
1 June	Balance b/d	2,450		

PRINCIPLES OF BOOKKEEPING CONTROLS

Sales account

	£			£
		5 May	Cash	300
		9 May	K Homes	300
			J Homes	300
31 May Balance c/d	1,000		B Hood	100
	1,000			1,000
		1 June	Balance b/d	1,000

Rates account

	£		£
6 May Bank	100	31 May Balance c/d	100
1 June Balance b/d	100		

Wages account

	£		£
8 May Cash	50		
26 May Bank	150	31 May Balance c/d	200
	200		200
1 June Balance b/d	200		

Purchase returns account

	£		£
31 May Balance c/d	150	11 May J Johnson	150
		1 June Balance b/d	150

Office fixtures account

	£		£
15 May Bank	600	31 May Balance c/d	600
1 June Balance b/d	600		

Motor vehicle account

	£		£
18 May Bank	3,500	31 May Balance c/d	3,500
1 June Balance b/d	3,500		

Sales returns account

	£		£
22 May J Homes	100	31 May Balance c/d	100
1 June Balance b/d	100		

Trial balance as at 30 May 20X6

	Dr £	Cr £
Cash	250	
Bank	950	
J Johnson		50
D Nixon		500
J Agnew		250
K Homes	300	
J Homes	200	
B Hood	100	
Capital		6,800
Purchases	2,450	
Sales		1,000
Rates	100	
Wages	200	
Purchase returns		150
Office fixtures	600	
Motor vehicles	3,500	
Sales returns	100	
	8,750	8,750

Test your understanding 12

Peter Wall

(a)

Cash

	£		£
Capital	10,000	Equipment	7,000
Loan	10,000	Ink	10
Revenue	200	Rent and rates	25
Receivables	60	Insurance	40
		Loan	400
		Loan interest	50
		Payables	200
		Payables	50
		Payables	100
		Balance c/d	12,385
	20,260		20,260
Balance b/d	12,385		

Payables

	£		£
Cash	200	Van	400
Cash	50	Purchases of paper	100
Cash	100		
Balance c/d	150		
	500		500
		Balance b/d	150

Capital

	£		£
		Cash	10,000

Loan account

	£		£
Cash	400	Cash	10,000
Balance c/d	9,600		
	10,000		10,000
		Balance b/d	9,600

Equipment

	£		£
Cash	7,000		

Van
	£		£
Payables (Arnold)	400		

Purchases of paper
	£		£
Payables (Butcher)	100		

Ink
	£		£
Cash	10		

Rent and rates
	£		£
Cash	25		

Loan interest
	£		£
Cash	50		

Insurance
	£		£
Cash	40		

Revenue
	£		£
Balance c/d	300	Cash	200
		Receivables (Constantine)	100
	300		300
		Balance b/d	300

Receivables
	£		£
Revenue	100	Cash	60
		Balance c/d	40
	100		100
Balance b/d	40		

(b) **Trial balance at 31 March 20X8**

	Debit £	Credit £
Cash	12,385	
Payables		150
Capital		10,000
Loan		9,600
Equipment	7,000	
Van	400	
Purchases of paper	100	
Purchases of ink	10	
Rent and rates	25	
Loan interest	50	
Insurance	40	
Revenue		300
Receivables	40	
	20,050	20,050

PRINCIPLES OF BOOKKEEPING CONTROLS

Control accounts and reconciliations

Introduction

This chapter considers three key control accounts: the receivables ledger control account, payables ledger control account and the VAT control account.

The receivables and payables ledger control accounts will be reconciled to the list of individual customer or supplier account balances in the subsidiary ledgers.

Finally the VAT control account will be used to determine whether the closing balance is a liability due to, or an amount receivable due from, the tax authorities.

ASSESSMENT CRITERIA	CONTENTS
Produce control accounts (1.1) Reconcile control accounts (1.2)	1 Accounting for receivables 2 Receivable ledger control account reconciliation 3 Accounting for payables 4 Payables ledger control account reconciliation 5 Identifying the reason for reconciliation differences 6 The VAT control account

1 Accounting for receivables

1.1 Introduction

Within the general ledger, the total amount outstanding from receivables is shown in the receivables ledger control account.

The totals of credit sales (from the sales day book), returns from customers (from the sales returns day book), cash received (from the analysed cash book) and discounts allowed (from the discounts allowed day book) are posted to this account. This account therefore shows the total receivables outstanding. It does not give details about individual customers' balances. This detail is available in the receivables ledger, which is also known as the receivables subsidiary ledger, a memorandum account.

However, as both records are compiled from the same sources, the total balances on the individual customers' accounts should equal the outstanding balance on the control account at any time.

1.2 Double-entry system

The double-entry system operates as follows.

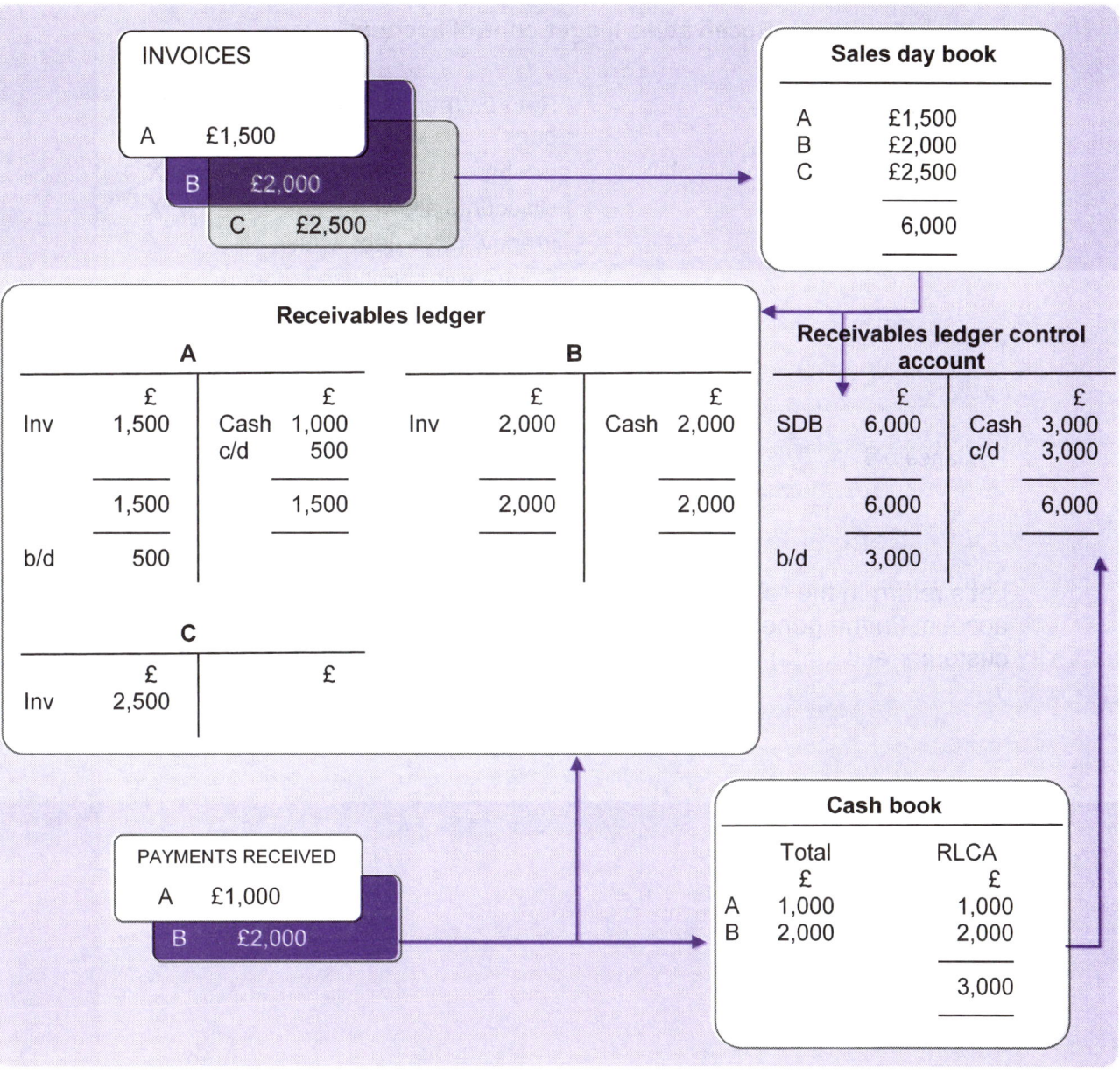

Notice that the remaining balance on the control account (£3,000) is equal to the sum of the remaining balances on the individual receivables' accounts (A £500 + C £2,500).

If all of the accounting entries have been made correctly, then the balance on the receivables ledger control account should equal the total of the balances in the receivables ledger (the sum of all the individual customer accounts).

1.3 Pro-forma receivables ledger control account

A receivables ledger control account can include the following:

Receivables ledger control account			
	£		£
Balance b/d	X	Returns (per sales returns day book)	X
Sales (per sales day book)	X	Cash from receivables	X
		Discounts allowed	X
		Irrecoverable debt written off	X
		Contra with purchase ledger	X
		Balance c/d	X
	X		X
Balance b/d			

1.4 General ledger and receivables ledger

Let's return to the relationship between the receivables ledger control account (in the general ledger) and the receivables ledger (the individual customer accounts).

PRINCIPLES OF BOOKKEEPING CONTROLS

 Example 1

Ayla has been trading for two months and is not registered for VAT. Ayla has four credit customers. Here are Ayla's sales day book and cash receipts book for the first two months:

Sales day book (SDB)

Date	Customer	Invoice	£
02.2.X4	Avery Brown	01	50.20
05.2.X4	Ian Smith	02	80.91
07.2.X4	Saeed Kara	03	73.86
23.2.X4	Eva Lane	04	42.30
	Total		247.27
09.3.X4	Ian Smith	05	23.96
15.3.X4	Saeed Kara	06	34.72
20.3.X4	Avery Brown	07	12.60
24.3.X4	Saeed Kara	08	93.25
31.3.X4	Total		164.53

Here is the receipts side of the analysed cash book for March 20X4 (no cash was received from receivables in February).

Cash receipts book (CRB)

Date	Narrative	Total	Cash sales	Receivables ledger	Rent
		£	£	£	£
01.3.X4	Avery Brown	50.20		50.20	
03.3.X4	Clare Jones	63.80	63.80		
04.3.X4	Molly Dell	110.00			110.00
12.3.X4	Saeed Kara	50.00		50.00	
13.3.X4	Emily Boyd	89.33	89.33		
20.3.X4	Frank Field	92.68	92.68		
25.3.X4	Eva Lane	42.30		42.30	
31.3.X4	Total	498.31	245.81	142.50	110.00

Let's write up the receivables ledger and the receivables ledger control account and compare the balances.

Solution

Receivables ledger – receivables

Avery Brown

		£			£
02.2.X4	01	50.20	28.2.X4	Balance c/d	50.20
		50.20			50.20
01.3.X4	Balance b/d	50.20	01.3.X4	Cash	50.20
20.3.X4	07	12.60	31.3.X4	Balance c/d	12.60
		62.80			62.80
01.4.X4	Balance b/d	12.60			

Eva Lane

		£			£
23.2.X4	04	42.30	28.2.X4	Balance c/d	42.30
		42.30			42.30
01.3.X4	Balance b/d	42.30	25.3.X4	Cash	42.30

Saeed Kara

		£			£
07.2.X4	03	73.86	28.2.X4	Balance c/d	73.86
		73.86			73.86
01.3.X4	Balance b/d	73.86	12.3.X4	Cash	50.00
15.3.X4	06	34.72	31.3.X4	Balance c/d	151.83
24.3.X4	08	93.25			
		201.83			201.83
01.4.X4	Balance b/d	151.83			

PRINCIPLES OF BOOKKEEPING CONTROLS

Ian Smith

		£			£
05.2.X4	02	80.91	28.2.X4	Balance c/d	80.91
		80.91			80.91
01.3.X4	Balance b/d	80.91	31.3.X4	Balance c/d	104.87
09.3.X4	05	23.96			
		104.87			104.87
01.4.X4	Balance b/d	104.87			

Receivables ledger control account

		£			£
28.2.X4	SDB	247.27	28.2.X4	Balance c/d	247.27
		247.27			247.27
01.3.X4	Balance b/d	247.27	31.3.X4	CRB	142.50
31.3.X4	SDB	164.53	31.3.X4	Balance c/d	269.30
		411.80			411.80
01.4.X4	Balance b/d	269.30			

Now compare balances at 31 March 20X4.

Subsidiary ledger – receivables

	£
Avery Brown	12.60
Eva Lane	–
Saeed Kara	151.83
Ian Smith	104.87
	269.30
Receivables ledger control account	269.30

As the double-entry has been correctly carried out, the total of the balances on the individual receivables' accounts in the receivables ledger is equal to the balance on the receivables ledger control account.

1.5 Irrecoverable debts

Definition

An irrecoverable debt is a debt relating to a receivable which is not going to be received. It is therefore not prudent for the business to consider this debt as an asset.

To prevent irrecoverable debts, it is important for the business to maintain an aged receivables listing.

An aged receivables listing is an extremely useful tool to the business. As well as highlighting balances which are overdue, it will also identify customers who are regularly paying late. This information will help the business become more efficient in collecting outstanding balances, which will in turn improve cash flow.

1.6 Reasons for irrecoverable debts

A business may decide that a debt is irrecoverable for a number of reasons:

- Customer is in liquidation – no cash will be received.
- Customer is having difficulty paying (although not officially in liquidation).
- Customer disputes the debt and refuses to pay all or part of it.

1.7 Accounting for irrecoverable debts

The business must make an adjustment to write off the irrecoverable debt from the customer's account in the receivables ledger and also to remove it from the general ledger. The double-entry in the general ledger is:

Dr   Irrecoverable debt expense

   Cr   Receivables ledger control account

Notice that the irrecoverable debt becomes an expense of the business, but is not deducted from sales. The sale was made in anticipation of receiving payment, but if the debt is not received, this does not negate the sale. It is just an added expense of the business.

The irrecoverable debt must also be written off in the individual customer's account in the receivables ledger. This write off is achieved by crediting the customer's account, which reduces the amount outstanding.

If the business is registered for VAT, the VAT payable on the sale will have been recorded and subsequently paid to the tax authorities (HMRC).

PRINCIPLES OF BOOKKEEPING CONTROLS

Once the debt is **more than 6 months old** and it has been determined that the customer is not going to pay, the business can reclaim that VAT back from the tax authorities. The adjusting journal is then:

Dr	Irrecoverable debt expense	Net amount
Dr	VAT control account	VAT amount
	Cr Receivables ledger control account	Gross amount

1.8 Contra entries

A further type of adjustment that may be required to receivables ledger and payables ledger control accounts is a contra entry.

Occasionally reciprocal trading arises, where a business both buys from and sells to another business, resulting in both a receivable and a payable balance with the same organisation. Rather than entering into 2 separate cash transaction to be made, it can be simplified by netting off the outstanding amounts. This adjustment is known as a contra entry.

Debit	Payables	x
Credit	Receivables	x

Example 2

Bechelli Associates has a customer, Xavier. Xavier also sells goods to Bechelli Associates. Therefore Xavier is both a customer and a supplier of Bechelli Associates. The subsidiary ledger accounts of Bechelli Associates show the following position:

Receivables ledger

Xavier

	£		£
Balance b/d	250		

Payables ledger

Xavier

	£		£
		Balance b/d	100

Xavier owes Bechelli Associates £250 and is owed £100 by Bechelli Associates. If both parties are in agreement, it makes more sense to net these two amounts off leaving Xavier owing Bechelli Associates just £150. This is achieved by a contra entry.

Control accounts and reconciliations: Chapter 2

Solution

Step 1 Take the smaller of the two amounts and debit the payables ledger account and credit the receivables ledger account with this amount.

Receivables ledger – receivables

Xavier

	£		£
Balance b/d	250	Contra	100

Payables ledger – payables

Xavier

	£		£
Contra	100	Balance b/d	100

Step 2 Balance off the accounts in the subsidiary ledgers.

Receivables ledger – receivables

Xavier

	£		£
Balance b/d	250	Contra	100
		Balance c/d	150
	250		250
Balance b/d	150		

Payables ledger – payables

Xavier

	£		£
Contra	100	Balance b/d	100

This now shows that Bechelli Associates is owed £150 from, and owes nothing to, Xavier

PRINCIPLES OF BOOKKEEPING CONTROLS

Step 3 The double-entry must also be carried out in the general ledger accounts. This is:

    Dr   Payables ledger control account

    Cr   Receivables ledger control account

When a contra entry is made deal with the entries in the subsidiary ledgers and post the double entry to the receivables ledger control account and payables ledger control accounts in the general ledger.

2 Receivables ledger control account reconciliation

2.1 Introduction

Comparing the receivables ledger control account balance with the total of the receivables ledger accounts is a form of internal control. The reconciliation should be performed on a regular basis by the receivables ledger clerk, then reviewed and approved by an independent person.

If the total of the balances on the receivables ledger does not equal the balance on the receivables ledger control account, then an error or errors have been made in the general ledger and/or receivables ledger, and these must be investigated and corrected.

Control accounts and reconciliations: **Chapter 2**

2.2 Journal entries

Chapter 1 introduced how a journal can be used to enter opening balances to start a new period of accounts. Journal entries are also used for unusual items that do not appear in the primary records, for the correction of errors or for adjusting ledger accounts.

A typical journal entry to write off an irrecoverable debt is shown below:

Authorisation →

Description of why double-entry is necessary →

Double-entry →

Sequential journal number

Equal totals as journal must balance

JOURNAL ENTRY		No: 06671		
Prepared by:	P Freer			
Authorised by:	P Simms			
Date:	3 October 20X2			
Narrative:				
To write off irrecoverable debt from L C Hamper				
Account		Code	Debit	Credit
Irrecoverable debts expense		GL28	102.00	
Receivables control (RLCA)		GL06		102.00
TOTALS			102.00	102.000

Example 3

The total sales for the month were posted from the sales day book as £4,657.98 instead of £4,677.98. This must be corrected using a journal entry.

Solution

The journal entry to correct this error will be as follows:

JOURNAL ENTRY		No: 97		
Prepared by:	A Gramma			
Authorised by:	L R Ridinghood			
Date:	23.7.X3			
Narrative:				
To correct error in posting from SDB				
Account		Code	Debit	Credit
Receivables ledger control		GL11	20	
Sales		GL56		20
TOTALS			20	20

The adjustment required is to increase receivables and sales by £20. A debit to receivables ledger control and a credit to sales is needed.

2.3 Adjustments in the subsidiary ledger

Adjustments in the subsidiary ledger do not need to be shown in a journal entry. Journal entries are only required for adjustments to the general ledger.

These adjustments should be recorded in memorandum form, with proper authorisation.

2.4 Procedure for a receivables ledger control account reconciliation

1. The balances on the receivables ledger accounts for receivables are extracted, listed and totalled.
2. The receivables ledger control account is balanced.
3. If the two figures differ, then the reasons for the difference must be investigated.

   Reasons may include the following:

   - error in the casting of the day book (the total is posted to the control account whereas the individual invoices are posted to the individual accounts, so if the total is incorrect a difference will arise)
   - transposition error (the figures are switched around, e.g. £87 posted as £78). This error could be made in either posting to the control account (from the day book total figure) or to the individual accounts (from the individual transactions)
   - casting error in the cash book column relating to the control account (total posted to control account, individual receipts to individual ledger accounts)
   - balance omitted from the list of individual accounts
   - credit balance on an individual account in the receivables ledger wrongly assumed to be a debit balance.

4. Differences which are errors in the control account only should be corrected directly within the control account.
5. Differences which are errors in the individual accounts only should be corrected by adjusting the account concerned and the list of balances.

Test your understanding 1

Would the following errors cause a difference to occur between the balance of the receivables ledger control account and the total of the balances in the receivables ledger?

(a) The total column of the sales day book was overcast by £100.

(b) £175 was debited in error to H Lambert's account in the receivables ledger instead of M Lambert's account.

(c) An invoice for £76 was recorded in the sales day book as £67.

PRINCIPLES OF BOOKKEEPING CONTROLS

 Example 4

The balance on the receivables ledger control account for a business at 31 March 20X3 is £14,378.37. The total of the list of receivables ledger balances for receivables is £13,935.37.

The difference has been investigated and the following errors have been identified:

- the sales day book was overcast by £1,000
- a credit note for £150 was entered into an individual customer's account as an invoice
- discounts allowed of £143 were correctly accounted for in the receivables ledger but were not entered into the general ledger accounts
- a credit balance on one customer's account of £200 was mistakenly listed as a debit balance when totalling the individual receivable accounts in the receivables ledger.

Prepare the reconciliation between the balance on the receivables ledger control account and the total of the individual balances on the receivables ledger accounts.

Solution

Step 1 Amend the receivables ledger control account for any errors that have been made.

Receivables ledger control account

	£		£
Balance b/d	14,378.37	SDB overcast	1,000.00
		Discounts allowed	143.00
		Balance c/d	13,235.37
	14,378.37		14,378.37
Balance b/d	13,235.37		

Step 2 Correct the total of the list of balances in the receivables ledger.

	£
Original total	13,935.37
Less: Credit note entered as invoice (2 × 150)	(300.00)
Credit balance entered as debit balance (2 × 200)	(400.00)
	13,235.37

Test your understanding 2

The balance on Diana's receivables ledger control account at 31 December 20X6 was £15,450. The balances on the individual accounts in the receivables ledger have been extracted and total £15,705. On investigation, the following errors are discovered:

(a) a debit balance of £65 has been omitted from the list of balances

(b) discounts totalling £70 have been recorded in the individual accounts but not in the control account

(c) the sales day book was 'overcast' by £200

(d) a contra entry for £40 has not been entered into the control account, and

(e) an invoice for £180 was recorded correctly in the sales day book but was posted to the customer's individual account as £810.

Prepare the receivables ledger control account reconciliation.

Test your understanding 3

The balance on the receivables ledger control account for a business at 30 June 20X2 is £18,971.12. The total of the list of subsidiary ledger balances for receivables is £21,761.12. The difference has been investigated and the following errors have been identified:

(a) The sales day book was undercast by £1,500.

(b) An invoice for £300 was entered twice into the subsidiary receivables ledger.

(c) Discounts allowed of £143 were entered in the receivables ledger control account as £133. They were correctly entered in the subsidiary receivables ledger.

(d) A credit note for £1,000 was omitted from one customer's account, although it was correctly entered in the general ledger.

Correct any errors in the receivables ledger control account and prepare the reconciliation between the corrected receivables ledger control accountant the total of the subsidiary receivables ledger..

 Test your understanding 4

The balance on the receivables ledger control account of Robin & Co on 30 September 20X0 amounted to £3,825 which did not agree with the net total of the list of receivables ledger balances at that date of £3,362.

The errors discovered were as follows:

1. Debit balances in the receivables ledger, amounting to £103, had been omitted from the list of balances.

2. An irrecoverable debt amounting to £400 had been written off in the receivables ledger but had not been posted to the irrecoverable debts expense account or entered in the control accounts.

3. An invoice for £250 for goods sold to Sparrow had been entered once in the sales day book but posted to the customer's individual account twice.

4. No entry had been made in the control account in respect of the transfer of a debit of £70 from Quail's account in the receivables ledger to Quail's account in the payables ledger (a contra entry).

5. The discount allowed column in the discount allowed daybook had been undercast by £140.

Control accounts and reconciliations: **Chapter 2**

Required:

(a) Make the necessary adjustments in the receivables ledger control account and bring down the balance.

(b) Show the adjustments to the net total of the original list of balances to reconcile with the amended balance on the receivables ledger control account.

3 Accounting for payables

3.1 Introduction

The total amount payable to suppliers is recorded in the general ledger within the payables ledger control account. The total of credit purchases (from the purchases day book), returns to suppliers (from the purchases returns day book), total payments to payables (from the cash payments book) and discounts received (taken from the discounts received daybook) are all posted to this account.

The payables ledger control account shows the total amount that is payable to suppliers but it does not show the amount owed to individual suppliers. This information is provided by the payables ledger which contains an account for each individual supplier.

Each individual invoice, credit note, payment and discount received from the day books are posted to the relevant supplier's account in the payables ledger.

3.2 Relationship between the payables ledger control account and the balances in the payables ledger

The information posted to the payables ledger control account and to the individual accounts in the payables ledger are from the same sources and should be the same figures in total.

PRINCIPLES OF BOOKKEEPING CONTROLS

3.3 Pro-forma payables ledger control account

A payables ledger control account normally includes the following transactions:

Payables ledger control account			
	£		£
Payments to suppliers (per cash book)	X	Balance b/d	X
Discount received (per discount received day book)	X	Purchases (per purchases day book)	X
Returns (per purchases returns day book)	X		
Contra with receivables ledger	X		
Balance c/d	X		
	X		X
		Balance b/d	X

If all of the accounting entries have been correctly made then the balance on this payables ledger control account should equal the total of the balances on the individual supplier accounts in the payables ledger.

Control accounts and reconciliations: **Chapter 2**

4 Payables ledger control account reconciliation

4.1 Introduction

At each month end, the payables ledger clerk must reconcile the payables ledger control account and the payables ledger.

Remember that, as well as investigating and discovering the differences, the control account and the individual accounts in the payables ledger must also be amended for any errors.

4.2 Adjustments to the payables ledger control account

Any corrections or adjustments made to the payables ledger control account can be documented as a journal entry.

Example 5

The total purchases for the month were posted from the purchases day book as £2,547.98 instead of £2,457.98. Prepare a journal to correct this error.

Solution

The journal entry to correct this error will be as follows:

JOURNAL ENTRY		No: 253		
Prepared by:	P Charming			
Authorised by:	A Sister			
Date:	29.8.X5			
Narrative:				
To correct the error in posting from the purchases day book				
Account		Code	Debit	Credit
Payables ledger control		GL56	90	
Purchases		GL34		90
TOTALS			90	90

In this case both PLCA and purchases need to be reduced by £90. Therefore, a debit to the payables ledger control and a credit to purchases are required.

4.3 Adjustments in the payables ledger

Adjustments in the payables ledger do not need to be documented in a journal entry. Journal entries are only required for adjustments to the general ledger.

Example 6

The balance on the payables ledger control account for a business at 30 June was £12,159. The total of the balances on the in the payables ledger was £19,200.

The following errors were also found:

- the cash payments book had been undercast by £20
- an invoice from Thomas Ltd, a credit supplier, for £2,400 was correctly entered in the payables ledger but had been missed out of the total in the purchases day book
- an invoice from Fred Singleton for £2,000 plus VAT was included in Fred's individual account in the payables ledger at the net amount
- an invoice from Horace Shades for £6,000 was entered in the payables ledger twice
- the same invoice is for £6,000 plus sales tax but the VAT had not been included in the payables ledger
- returns to Horace Shades of £261 had been omitted from the payables ledger.

You are required to reconcile the payables ledger control account with the balances on the payables ledger accounts at 30 June.

Solution

Step 1 Amend the payables ledger control account to show the correct balance.

Payables ledger control account

	£		£
Undercast of CPB	20	Balance b/d	12,159
Balance c/d	14,539	Invoice omitted from PDB	2,400
	14,559		14,559
		Amended balance b/d	14,539

Step 2 Correct the total of the list of payables ledger balances.

	£
Original total	19,200
Add: Fred Singleton VAT	400
Less: Horace Shades invoice included twice	(6,000)
Add: Horace Shades VAT	1,200
Less: Horace Shades returns	(261)
Amended total of list of balances	14,539

Remember that invoices from suppliers should be included in the payables ledger at the gross amount including VAT.

Test your understanding 5

The following totals are taken from the books of a business:

	£
Credit balance on payables ledger control account	5,926
Debit balance on receivables ledger control account	10,268
Credit sales	71,504
Credit purchases	47,713
Cash received from credit customers	69,872
Cash paid to payables	47,028
Receivables ledger balances written off as irrecoverable	96
Sales returns	358
Purchases returns	202
Discounts allowed	1,435
Discounts received	867
Contra entry	75

Required:

(a) Prepare the payables ledger control account and balance at the end of the month.

(b) Prepare the receivables ledger control account and balance at the end of the month.

PRINCIPLES OF BOOKKEEPING CONTROLS

Test your understanding 6

How would each of the following be dealt with in the payables ledger control account reconciliation?

(a) A purchase invoice for £36 from P Swift credited to P Short's account in the subsidiary ledger.

(b) A purchase invoice for £96 not entered in the purchases day book.

(c) An undercast of £20 in the total column of the purchases day book.

(d) A purchase invoice from Short & Long for £42 entered as £24 in the purchases day book.

Test your understanding 7

When carrying out the payables ledger control account reconciliation002C the following errors were discovered:

(a) the purchases day book was overcast by £1,000

(b) the total of the discount received column in the discounts received daybook was posted to the general ledger as £89 instead of £98

(c) a contra entry of £300 had been entered in the subsidiary ledger but not in the general ledger.

Required:

Produce journal entries to correct each of these errors.

5 Identifying the reason for reconciliation differences

5.1 Introduction

Within the POBC assessment, you may be asked to suggest what may have caused the difference between the control account and the list of balances.

An example of such a task is shown below:

Example 7

XYZ Ltd has made the following entries in the receivables ledger control account in April 20X7.

	£
Opening balance 1 April 20X7	49,139
Credit sales posted from the sales day book	35,000
Discounts allowed	328
Irrecoverable debt written off	127
Cash received from customers	52,359

The list of balances from the receivables ledger totals £31,579.

(a) Calculate the closing balance on the RLCA at 30 April 20X7.

(b) State one possible reason for the difference between the RLCA balance and the total of the list of balances.

Solution

(a) The RLCA

Receivables ledger control account

	£		£
Balance b/d	49,139	Discount allowed	328
SDB – sales	35,000	Irrecoverable debt	127
		Cash received	52,359
		Balance c/d	31,325
	84,139		84,139

(b)
Total of receivables ledger balances	31,579
Balance of RLCA at 30 April 20X7	(31,325)
Difference	254

Note

To suggest a valid reason for the difference, look for any obvious clues but also feel free to make relevant assumptions

(i) It's reasonable to assume that the control account is correct – unless further details are provided that indicate it is not

PRINCIPLES OF BOOKKEEPING CONTROLS

(ii) Calculate the difference and determine whether the receivable ledger total is larger than the RLCA balance or vice versa.

(iii) See if one of the figures given in the question is the same as the difference or double the difference.

If a figure given in the question details is the same as the difference, then it is likely that a transaction has been left out of the RLCA or the receivables ledger.

If the difference is double a figure given in the details, then it is likely that a transaction has been entered on the wrong side of an account, or possibly entered twice.

- In the above question, the difference is £254.
- The total of the list of ledger balances is bigger than the RLCA balance.
- £254 does not equal any of the transactions provided in the question but the difference is twice the irrecoverable debt written off of £127.

One possible reason for the difference is that the irrecoverable debt write off (£127) was entered on the debit side of a ledger account in the receivables ledger – that would have made the total of the list £254 larger.

There are many other possible reasons that could have caused the difference (e.g. perhaps an invoice for £254 was entered twice in a receivables ledger account), however the assessment question will be looking for a reason that is apparent from the figures given, rather than a speculative reason.

Test your understanding 8

Show whether each entry will be a debit or credit in the receivables ledger control account in the general ledger:

TRANSACTION	Amount (£)	DEBIT ✓	CREDIT ✓
Balance brought down	60,980		
Goods sold on credit	12,566		
Returns made by credit customers	4,224		
Payments made by credit customers	15,789		
Discounts allowed	569		
Irrecoverable debt written off	872		

What will be the balance carried down?

The following balances were identified in the subsidiary ledgers:

COMPANY	£
ABC Ltd	14,600 Dr
Shoebox Ltd	7,860 Dr
Heels R Us	12,500 Dr
Feet First Ltd	10,043 Dr
Twinkle Toes plc	7,961 Dr

Reconcile the balance on the control account to the balance per the subsidiary ledgers.

Balance on control account:

Balance per subsidiary ledgers:

Difference:

What may have caused the difference between the control account and the subsidiary ledgers?

(a) Discounts allowed may have been omitted from the subsidiary ledger.

(b) Discounts allowed may have been omitted from the control account.

(c) Irrecoverable debts may have been omitted from the subsidiary ledger.

(d) Irrecoverable debts may have been omitted from the control account.

PRINCIPLES OF BOOKKEEPING CONTROLS

6 The VAT control account

6.1 Introduction

The calculation of VAT chargeable on sales, and the VAT reclaimable on purchases has previously been covered within Introduction to Bookkeeping.

The POBC syllabus now considers how these transactions would be recorded within the VAT control account, and that the VAT control account balance must be paid to or received from the tax authorities (HMRC).

In the assessment, candidates must be able to process the entries and verify whether the balance represents a liability due to, or an asset due from, HMRC.

Example 8

The following VAT figures have been extracted from a business' day books. Complete the VAT control account, and find the balance.

Sales day book	22,436
Sales returns day book	674
Purchases day book	15,327

Solution

VAT account

Details	Amount £	Details	Amount £
Sales returns (SRDB)	674	Sales (SDB)	22,436
Purchases (PDB)	15,327		
Balance c/d	6,435		
	22,436		**22,436**

The VAT from the sales day book is payable to HMRC, whereas the VAT from the sales returns and the purchases day books can be reclaimed. It is the net amount that is payable to HMRC.

Businesses are required to complete a VAT return, usually on a quarterly basis, to show the amount payable to or reclaimed from HMRC. Although assessment candidates will not be required to complete the return itself, it is possible to be provided with the amount on the completed VAT return and be asked to confirm it to the VAT control account calculated.

Test your understanding 9

This quarter Sasha had net sales of £189,500, made purchases inclusive of VAT of £240,000 and received returns from customers amounting to £1,880 excluding VAT.

Draw up the VAT control account for Sasha, stating clearly whether the closing balance is payable to or receivable from HMRC.

Test your understanding 10

The following VAT figures have been extracted from the books of prime entry.

Sales day book	60,200
Sales returns day book	980
Purchases day book	34,300
Purchases returns day book	2,660
Cash receipts book	112
Discounts allowed day book	640
Discounts received day book	450

(a) Show the entries in the VAT control account to record the VAT transactions in the quarter.

(b) The VAT return has been completed and shows an amount owing from the tax authorities of £27,502. Is the VAT return correct?

7 Summary

This chapter has looked at control account reconciliations. The entries into the RLCA and PLCA are items that students should be comfortable with. However the process of reconciling the control accounts to the subsidiary ledgers can be tricky. The reconciliation requires knowledge of the impacts of errors of the different accounts. It is important to be comfortable with the types of errors that could arise.

For the VAT control account, candidates must be able to process VAT entries and to verify whether the balance represents a liability due to, or an asset due from, HMRC.

Test your understanding answers

Test your understanding 1

(a) Yes, because the correct entries in the sales day book are posted to the receivables ledger and the incorrect total used in the control account.

(b) No, because the arithmetical balance is correct.

(c) No, because the total posted to the RLCA will include the £67 and the entry in the receivables ledger will also be for £67.

Test your understanding 2

- Firstly identify those errors which will mean that the RLCA is incorrectly stated. The control account is then adjusted as follows:

Receivables ledger control account

	£		£
Balance b/d	15,450	Discounts allowed	70
		Overcast of sales day book	200
		Contra with PLCA	40
		Adjusted balance c/d	15,140
	15,450		15,450
Balance b/d	15,140		

- Then identify errors in the total of individual balances per the receivables ledger. The list of balances must be adjusted as follows:

Original total of the list of balances	15,705
Debit balance omitted	65
Transposition error (810 – 180)	(630)
	15,140

- The adjusted total of the list of balances now agrees with the balance on the control account.

PRINCIPLES OF BOOKKEEPING CONTROLS

Test your understanding 3

- Identify those errors that cause the receivables ledger control account to be incorrectly stated. The control account is then adjusted as follows:

Receivables ledger control account

	£		£
Balance b/d	18,971.12	Discounts allowed	10.00
Undercast of sales day book	1,500.00		
		Adjusted balance c/d	20,461.12
	20,471.12		20,471.12
Balance b/d	20,461.12		

- Then identify errors in the total of the individual balances in the receivables ledger. The extracted list of balances must be adjusted as follows:

	£
Original total of the list of balances	21,761.12
Invoice duplication	(300.00)
Omission of credit note	(1,000.00)
	20,461.12

- The adjusted total of the list of balances now agrees with the balance on the control account.

Test your understanding 4

(a)   **Receivables ledger control account**

	£		£
30 Sep Balance b/d	3,825	Irrecoverable debts (2)	400
		PLCA (4)	70
		Discount allowed (5)	140
		Balance c/d	3,215
	3,825		3,825
1 Oct Balance b/d	3,215		

(b) **List of receivables ledger balances**

	£
Original total	3,362
Add: Debit balances previously omitted (1)	103
	3,465
Less: Item posted twice to Sparrow's account (3)	(250)
Amended total agreeing with RLCA	3,215

Test your understanding 5

(a)

Payables ledger control account

	£		£
Cash paid	47,028	Balance b/d	5,926
Purchases returns	202	Purchases (total from PDB)	47,713
Discounts received	867		
Receivables ledger control account (contra)	75		
Balance c/d (bal fig)	5,467		
	53,639		53,639

(b)

Receivables ledger control account

	£		£
Balance b/d	10,268	Cash received (CRB)	69,872
Sales (SDB)	71,504	Irrecoverable debts account	96
		Sales returns account (total from SRDB)	358
		Discounts allowed	1,435
		Payables ledger control account (contra)	75
		Balance c/d (bal fig)	9,936
	81,772		81,772

Test your understanding 6

(a) An incorrectly posted invoice between subsidiary ledger accounts does not affect the reconciliation. A correction would be made in the subsidiary ledger.

(b) An omitted transaction from the PDB must be adjusted for in the purchase ledger control account and in the payables ledger.

(c) An undercast column in the PDB just needs an adjustment to the purchase ledger control account.

(d) A transposition error entered in the PDB will require alteration in both the control account and the payables ledger.

Test your understanding 7

(a)

Account name	Amount £	Dr ✓	Cr ✓
Payables ledger control account	1,000.00	✓	
Purchases	1,000.00		✓

(b)

Account name	Amount £	Dr ✓	Cr ✓
Payables ledger control account	9.00	✓	
Discounts received	9.00		✓

(c)

Account name	Amount £	Dr ✓	Cr ✓
Payables ledger control account	300.00	✓	
Receivables ledger control account	300.00		✓

PRINCIPLES OF BOOKKEEPING CONTROLS

Test your understanding 8

TRANSACTION	Amount (£)	DEBIT ✓	CREDIT ✓
Balance brought down	60,980	✓	
Goods sold on credit	12,566	✓	
Returns made by credit customers	4,224		✓
Payments made by credit customers	15,789		✓
Discounts allowed	569		✓
Irrecoverable debt written off	872		✓

The balance carried down will be **£52,092**

Balance per control account: £52,092

Balance per subsidiary ledgers: £52,964

Difference: £872

The difference may have been caused by irrecoverable debts being omitted from the subsidiary ledger, meaning that the subsidiary ledger is £872 higher than the control account.

Test your understanding 9

(a) **VAT account**

Details	Amount £	Details	Amount £
Purchases	40,000	Sales	37,900
Sales returns	376		
		Balance c/d	2,476
	40,376		40,376
Balance b/d	2,476		

(b) The amount of £2,476 is reclaimable from the tax authorities.

Test your understanding 10

(a) **VAT account**

Details	Amount £	Details	Amount £
Sales Returns (SRDB)	980	Sales (SDB)	60,200
Purchases (PDB)	34,300	Purchases returns	2,660
Discounts allowed day book	640	Cash sales (CRB)	112
		Discounts received	450
Balance c/d	27,502		
	63,422		**63,422**
		Balance b/d	27,502

(b) No. The amount of £27,502 is payable **to** the tax authorities.

PRINCIPLES OF BOOKKEEPING CONTROLS

Errors and suspense accounts

Introduction

When preparing an initial trial balance, it may be necessary to open a suspense account to deal with any errors. The suspense account is need when the Dr and Cr columns in the TB do not balance. The suspense account cannot be allowed to remain permanently in the trial balance, and must be cleared by correcting each of the errors causing the imbalance.

ASSESSMENT CRITERIA	CONTENTS
Produce journal entries to record bookkeeping transactions (3.1)	1 The journal
	2 Errors
Produce journal entries to correct errors not disclosed by the trial balance (3.2)	3 Opening a suspense account
	4 Clearing the suspense account
Produce journal entries to correct errors disclosed by the trial balance (3.3)	5 Re-drafting the trial balance
Re-draft the trial balance following adjustments (4.2)	

Errors and suspense accounts: Chapter 3

1 The journal

1.1 Introduction

The journal is used to process double entries that are not obtained from the other books of prime entry (such as the sales day book). Journals will be used regularly within the assessment, so it is important to understand their format and how to produce them.

Journals will either be used to process a new double entry, or to correct errors. The assessment will use journals for a variety of reasons, including opening balances, payroll transactions and late adjustments such as irrecoverable debts and contras.

Journals are an essential part of the bookkeeping system, and are vital in performing adjustments to ensure that the financial statements are produced accurately.

When journals are required, they should be completed accurately and quickly to avoid delays to the accounts being processed.

2 Errors

2.1 Introduction

One of the purposes of the trial balance is to provide a check on the accuracy of double-entry bookkeeping. If the trial balance does not balance, then an error or a number of errors have occurred and this must be investigated and the errors corrected.

2.2 Errors detected by the trial balance

The following types of error will cause a difference in, and therefore will be detected by, the trial balance and can be investigated and corrected:

A single entry – if only one side of a double entry has been made the trial balance will not balance e.g. if only the cash entry for receipts from receivables has been made then the debit total on the trial balance will exceed the credit balance.

A casting error – a casting error is where a list has been incorrectly totalled, or a ledger balance has been added incorrectly. If one account balance has been incorrectly totalled, or one side of the trial balance miscast, this will mean that the trial balance will not balance.

PRINCIPLES OF BOOKKEEPING CONTROLS

A transposition error – if an amount has been accidentally transposed (numbers have switched positions) and incorrectly recorded in one ledger account, then the trial balance will not balance e.g. a debit entry was recorded correctly as £5,276 but the related credit entry was entered as £5,726.

An extraction error – if a ledger account balance is incorrectly recorded on the trial balance either by recording the wrong figure or putting the balance on the wrong side of the trial balance, then the trial balance will not balance.

An omission error – if a ledger account balance is inadvertently omitted from the trial balance then the trial balance will not balance.

Two entries on one side – if a transaction is entered as two debits or two credits then the trial balance will not balance.

2.3 Errors not detected by the trial balance

It is important to prepare a trial balance to check on the accuracy of the double entry. However not all errors in the accounting system can be detected by preparing a trial balance.

This is because some errors will have an equal debit and credit.

An error of original entry – the wrong figure is entered as both the debit and credit entry e.g. a payment for electricity was correctly recorded as a debit in the electricity account and a credit to the bank account but it was recorded as £300 instead of £330 in both accounts.

A compensating error – two separate errors are made, one on the debit side of the accounts and the other on the credit side. By coincidence, the two errors are for the same amount and cancel each other out.

An error of omission – an entire double entry is omitted from the ledger accounts. As both the debit and credit have been omitted, the trial balance will still balance.

An error of commission – a debit entry and an equal credit entry have been made but one of the entries has been to the wrong account e.g. if the electricity expense was debited to the rent account but the credit entry was correctly made in the bank account – here both the electricity account and rent account will be incorrect but the trial balance will still balance.

An error of principle – this is similar to an error of commission but the entry has been made in the **wrong type** of account e.g. if a purchase of a motor vehicle was debited to motor expenses. Both the motor vehicle cost account and the motor expenses account would be incorrect but the trial balance would still balance.

2.4 Correction of errors

Errors will normally be corrected by using a journal. The procedure for correcting errors is as follows:

Step 1 – What has been done?

Determine the incorrect double entry that has been made.

Step 2 – What should have been done?

Determine the correct entries that should have been made.

Step 3 – What needs to be done to correct it?

Produce a journal entry that reverses the incorrect parts and records the correct entries.

Example 1

The electricity expense of £450 has been correctly credited to the bank account but has been debited to the rent account.

Step 1 – What has been done?

Debit Rent £450, Credit Bank £450

Step 2 – What should have been done?

Debit Electricity £450, Credit Bank £450

Step 3 – What needs to be done to correct it?

The journal entry required is:

Dr   Electricity   £450
Cr   Rent   £450

Note that this removes the incorrect debit from the rent account and puts the correct debit into the electricity account. No adjustment is necessary to the bank account, as this has been correctly credited.

Test your understanding 1

Colin returned some goods to a supplier because they were faulty. The original purchase price of these goods was £8,260.

The ledger clerk has correctly treated the double entry but used the figure £8,620.

What is the correcting entry?

PRINCIPLES OF BOOKKEEPING CONTROLS

3 Opening a suspense account

3.1 Introduction

A suspense account will be necessary when the trial balance totals do not balance e.g. due to errors such as only processing one side of an entry.

A suspense account is created as a temporary account to balance the trial balance. Using a suspense account means that, despite an error being present, it is possible to continue producing the financial accounts while the reasons for the errors are investigated and corrected.

In the assessment, it is likely that you will have to deal with a suspense account. You may be required to open up a suspense account in order to balance the trial balance, and then produce entries to clear the suspense account.

The method for clearing the suspense account is very similar to the steps outlined earlier for dealing with errors.

3.2 Reasons for opening a suspense account

A suspense account will be opened for two reasons:

(a) The bookkeeper does not know how to deal with one side of a transaction, or

(b) The trial balance does not balance.

3.3 Unknown entry

The bookkeeper may come across a transaction where they are uncertain of the correct double entry. The bookkeeper may choose to enter one side of the entry into a suspense account until the correct entry can be determined.

Example 2

Imani is a new bookkeeper who is dealing with a bank payment received from a garage for £800 for the sale of an old car. Imani correctly debits the bank account with the amount of the payment received, but does not know what to do with the credit entry.

Solution

Imani will enter it in the suspense account:

Suspense account

£		£
	Bank account – receipt from sale of car	800

Imani will investigate the issue, determine that the credit should have been posted to receivables, and then post the correction as Dr Suspense £800 Cr Receivables ledger control account £800. This correction will remove the suspense account.

3.4 Trial balance does not balance

If the total of the debits on the trial balance does not equal the total of the credits then errors have been made. These errors must be investigated, identified and corrected. In the meantime, the difference is inserted as a suspense account balance in order to balance the trial balance.

Example 3

The totals of a trial balance are as follows:

	Debits £	Credits £
Totals as initially extracted	108,367	109,444
Suspense account, to make the TB balance	1,077	
	109,444	109,444

Suspense

	£		£
Opening balance	1,077		

PRINCIPLES OF BOOKKEEPING CONTROLS

Test your understanding 2

The debit balances on a trial balance exceed the credit balances by £2,600. Open up a suspense account to record this difference.

Test your understanding 3

Which of the errors below are, or are not, disclosed by the trial balance? (Ignore VAT in all cases)

(a) Recording a receipt from a customer in the bank account only.

(b) Recording a bank payment of £56 for motor expenses as £65 in the expense account.

(c) Recording a credit purchase on the debit side of the payables ledger control account and the credit side of the purchases account.

(d) Recording a payment for electricity in the insurance account.

(e) Recording a bank receipt for cash sales on the credit side of both the bank and the sales account.

(f) Incorrectly calculating the balance on the motor vehicles account.

(g) Writing off an irrecoverable debt in the irrecoverable debt expense and receivables ledger control accounts only.

(h) An account with a ledger balance of £3,500 was recorded on the trial balance as £350.

4 Clearing the suspense account

4.1 Introduction

The suspense account is only ever a temporary account. The errors causing the suspense account must be identified and correcting entries processed to clear the suspense account to an overall nil balance, after which the TB will balance.

4.2 Procedure for clearing the suspense account

Step 1 – What has been done?

Determine the incorrect entry that has been made or the omission from the ledger accounts.

Step 2 – What should have been done?

Work out what the correct entry should have been.

Step 3 – What needs to be done to correct it?

This is the tricky part. Some adjustments will need to be made to the suspense account, and some will not.

Remember that if the initial entry, in step 1, did not balance, a suspense account will have been created and now needs to be cleared.

If the initial error balanced (step 1), no suspense account would have been created and therefore no adjustment is required to clear the suspense account.

When all the corrections have been made to the suspense account, the balance on the suspense account will be nil.

Example 4

A trial balance has been extracted and does not balance. The debit column totalled £200,139 and the credit column totalled £200,239.

You discover that cash purchases of £100 have been correctly entered into the cash account but no entry has been made in the purchases account.

Draft a journal entry to correct this error, and complete the suspense ledger account.

PRINCIPLES OF BOOKKEEPING CONTROLS

Solution

Step 1 – What has been done?

Dr

    Cr Cash   £100

As this does not balance, a **DEBIT** balance has been created on the suspense account of £100.

Suspense

Detail	Amount £	Detail	Amount £
TB	100		
	100		100

Step 2 – What should have been done?

The correct double entry should have been

Dr Purchases   £100

    Cr Cash   £100

Step 3 – What needs to be done to correct it?

A debit entry is required in the purchases account and the credit is to the suspense account.

Dr Purchases   £100   (To record the purchase)

    Cr Suspense   £100   (To remove the suspense)

Being correction of double entry for cash purchases.

Suspense

Detail	Amount £	Detail	Amount £
TB	100	Journal 1 (detailed above)	100
	100		100

Remember that normally a journal entry needs a narrative to explain what it is for. However in some assessment tasks you are told not to provide the narratives, so always read the requirements carefully.

Errors and suspense accounts: Chapter 3

 Example 5

On 31 December 20X0, the trial balance of Luis failed to agree and the difference of £967 was entered as a debit balance on the suspense account. After the final accounts had been prepared, the following errors were discovered and the difference was eliminated.

1. A purchase of goods from A Smith for £170 had been credited in error to the account of H Smith.
2. The purchases day book was undercast by £200.
3. Machinery purchased for £150 had been debited to the purchases account.
4. Discounts received of £130 had been posted to the debit of the discounts received account.
5. Rates paid by cheque for £46 had been posted to the debit of the rates account as £64.
6. Cash drawings by the owner of £45 had been entered in the cash account correctly but not posted to the drawings account.
7. A non-current asset balance of £1,200 had been omitted from the trial balance.

Required:

(a) Show the journal entries necessary to correct the above errors.

(b) Show the entries in the suspense account to eliminate the differences entered in the suspense account.

Note: The control accounts are part of the double entry.

Solution

Note that the errors do not have to affect the suspense account. Part of the way of dealing with these questions is to identify which entries do and do not affect the suspense account. Do not assume that all errors must be processed through the suspense account.

Journal – Luis

		Dr £	Cr £
31 December 20X0			
1	H Smith	170	
	A Smith		170
	Being adjustment of incorrect entry for purchases from A Smith – this correction takes place in the payables ledger (no effect on suspense account or general ledger)		
2	Purchases	200	
	Payables ledger control account		200
	Being correction of undercast of purchases day book (no effect on suspense account)		
3	Machinery	150	
	Purchases		150
	Being adjustment for wrong entry for machinery purchased (no effect on suspense account)		
4	Suspense account	260	
	Discount received		260
	Being correction of discounts entered on wrong side of account		
5	Suspense account	18	
	Rates		18
	Being correction of transposition error to rates account		
6	Drawings	45	
	Suspense account		45
	Being completion of double entry for drawings		
7	Non-current asset	1,200	
	Suspense account		1,200
	Being introduction of non-current asset balance.		

Errors and suspense accounts: Chapter 3

Suspense account

	£		£
Difference in trial balance	967	Drawings	45
Discounts received	260	Non-current asset per trial balance	1,200
Rates	18		
	1,245		1,245

Note that not all error corrections will require an entry to the suspense account.

Test your understanding 4

GA extracted the following trial balance from the ledgers at 31 May 20X4.

	£	£
Petty cash	20	
Capital		1,596
Drawings	1,400	
Sales		20,607
Purchases	15,486	
Purchases returns		210
Inventory (1 January 20X4)	2,107	
Fixtures and fittings	710	
Receivables ledger control	1,819	
Payables ledger control		2,078
Carriage on purchases	109	
Carriage on sales	184	
Rent and rates	460	
Light and heat	75	
Postage and telephone	91	
Sundry expenses	190	
Cash at bank	1,804	
	24,455	24,491

The trial balance did not agree. On investigation, GA discovered the following errors which had occurred during the month of May.

1. In extracting the receivables balance, the **credit** side of the receivables ledger control account had been overcast by £10.
2. An amount of £4 for carriage on sales had been posted in error to the carriage on purchases account.
3. A credit note for £17 received from a supplier had been entered in the purchase returns account but no entry had been made in the payables ledger control account.
4. £35 charged by Builders Ltd for repairs to GA's private residence had been charged in error to the sundry expenses account.
5. A payment of a telephone bill of £21 had been entered correctly in the cash book but had been posted in error to the postage and telephone account as £12.

Required:

(a) Create a suspense account to balance the trial balance.

(b) Using journal entries show what corrections are required in GA's ledger accounts and re-write the trial balance as it should appear after all the above corrections have been made. Show how the suspense account is cleared.

5 Re-drafting the trial balance

Once the suspense account has been cleared, it is important to re-draft the trial balance to ensure that the debit column and credit column agree.

Example 6

On 30 November, an initial trial balance was extracted which did not balance and a suspense account was opened. On 1 December journal entries were prepared to correct the errors that had been found and clear the suspense account. The list of balances and the journal entries are shown below.

Re-draft the trial balance by placing the figures in the debit or credit column, after taking into account the journal entries which will clear the suspense.

Errors and suspense accounts: Chapter 3

	Balances as at 30 November	Balances as at 1 December	
		Debit £	Credit £
Motor vehicles	10,500		
Inventory	2,497		
Bank overdraft	1,495		
Petty cash	162		
Receivables ledger control	6,811		
Payables ledger control	2,104		
VAT owing to HMRC	1,329		
Capital	15,000		
Sales	47,036		
Purchases	27,914		
Purchase returns	558		
Wages	12,000		
Motor expenses	947		
Drawings	6,200		
Suspense (debit balance)	491		

Journals

Account	Debit £	Credit £
Motor expenses		9
Suspense	9	
Being correction of transposition error when recording expense		

Account	Debit £	Credit £
Drawings	500	
Suspense		500
Being correction to analyse unknown cheque payment		

PRINCIPLES OF BOOKKEEPING CONTROLS

Solution

	Balances as at 30 November	Balances as at 1 December Debit £	Balances as at 1 December Credit £
Motor vehicles	10,500	10,500	
Inventory	2,497	2,497	
Bank overdraft	1,495		1,495
Petty cash	162	162	
Receivables ledger control	6,811	6,811	
Payables ledger control	2,104		2,104
VAT owing to HMRC	1,329		1,329
Capital	15,000		15,000
Sales	47,036		47,036
Purchases	27,914	27,914	
Purchase returns	558		558
Wages	12,000	12,000	
Motor expenses	947	**938**	
Drawings	6,200	**6,700**	
Suspense (debit balance)	491		
		67,522	67,522

The drawings and the motor expenses figures have been amended for the journals and the trial balance columns agree without the need for a suspense account.

Test your understanding 5

Luxury Caravans' initial trial balance includes a suspense account with a balance of £2,800 as shown below:

	£
Receivables	33,440
Bank (debit balance)	2,800
Sales	401,300
Inventory	24,300
Wages	88,400
Telephone	2,200
Motor car	12,000
VAT (credit balance)	5,300
Electricity	3,800
Rent	16,200
Purchases	241,180
Purchases returns	1,600
Sales returns	4,200
Office equipment	5,000
Capital	49,160
Motor expenses	5,040
Discounts allowed	4,010
Discounts received	2,410
Payables	20,000
Drawings	40,000
Suspense (credit balance)	2,800

The following errors have been discovered:

- Rent of £200 has been debited to the motor expenses account.

- An electricity payment of £800 has been debited to both the electricity and the bank account.

- The balance on the discounts received account has been incorrectly extracted to the TB – the actual balance on the ledger account was £4,210.

- The balance on the miscellaneous expenses account of £500 was omitted from the TB.

- The purchase returns day book for 22 May was incorrectly totalled, as shown below:

Purchase returns day book					
Date	Details	Credit note number	Total £	VAT £	Net £
22 May	Todd Ltd	578	120	20	100
22 May	Fallon Ltd	579	96	16	80
22 May	Dean's Plc	580	144	24	120
	Totals		360	160	300

Required:

(a) Produce journal entries to correct all of the above errors.

(b) Re-draft the trial balance using the balances above and your journal entries to show the suspense account has been cleared.

6 Summary

Preparation of the trial balance is an important element of control over the double-entry system but it will not detect all errors.

The trial balance will still balance if a number of types of error are made. If the trial balance does not balance then a suspense account will be opened temporarily to make the debits equal the credits in the trial balance.

The errors or omissions that have caused the difference on the trial balance must be investigated and then corrected using journal entries. Not all errors will require an entry to the suspense account. However, any that do, should be adjusted in the suspense account in order to eliminate the suspense balance.

Test your understanding answers

Test your understanding 1

Step 1

The payables ledger control account has been debited and the purchases returns account credited but with £8,620 rather than £8,260.

Step 2

Both of the entries need to be reduced by the difference between the amount used and the correct amount (8,620 – 8,260) = £360.

Step 3

Journal entry:	£	£
Dr Purchases returns account	360	
Cr Payables ledger control account		360

Being correction of misposting of purchases returns.

Test your understanding 2

As the debit balances exceed the credit balances, the balance needed is a credit balance to make the two totals equal.

Suspense account

	£		£
		Opening balance	2,600

PRINCIPLES OF BOOKKEEPING CONTROLS

> **Test your understanding 3**
>
> (a) Error disclosed by the trial balance – a single entry
> (b) Error disclosed by the trial balance – a transposition error
> (c) Error NOT disclosed by the trial balance – a reversal of entries
> (d) Error NOT disclosed by the trial balance – an error of commission
> (e) Error disclosed by the trial balance – two entries on one side
> (f) Error disclosed by the trial balance – a casting error
> (g) Error NOT disclosed by the trial balance – double entry is correct, it is only the subsidiary receivables ledger that hasn't been updated
> (h) Error disclosed by the trial balance – an extraction error

Test your understanding 4

(a) A suspense account will be opened with a DEBIT balance of £36, as the credit side of the TB is £36 larger than the debit side.

(b) See below.

What has been done?	What should have been done?	What should be done to correct it?
The credit side has been overcast, meaning that the receivable balance is UNDERSTATED by £10. Dr Suspense £10 Cr Receivables £10	Receivables should have been totalled to £1,829 rather than £1,819.	Dr Receivables £10 Cr Suspense £10
Dr Carriage on purchases £4 Cr Cash £4	Dr Carriage on sales £4 Cr Cash £4	Dr Carriage on sales £4 Cr Carriage on purchases £4
Dr Suspense £17 Cr Purchase returns £17	Dr PLCA £17 Cr Purchase returns £17	Dr PLCA £17 Cr Suspense £17
Dr Sundry expenses £35 Cr Cash £35	Dr Drawings £35 Cr Cash £35	Dr Drawings £35 Cr Sundry expenses £35
Dr Phone expense £12 Cr Cash £21 Dr Suspense £9	Dr Phone expense £21 Cr Cash £21	Dr Phone expense 9 Cr Suspense 9

			Dr £	Cr £
1	Debit	Receivables ledger control account	10	
	Credit	Suspense account		10
	Being correction of undercast in receivables ledger control account		
2	Debit	Carriage on sales	4	
	Credit	Carriage on purchases		4
	Being correction of wrong posting		
3	Debit	Payables ledger control account	17	
	Credit	Suspense account		17
	Being correction of omitted entry		
4	Debit	Drawings	35	
	Credit	Sundry expenses		35
	Being payment for private expenses		
5	Debit	Postage and telephone	9	
	Credit	Suspense account		9
	Being correction of transposition error		

Suspense account

	£		£
Difference per trial balance (24,455 – 24,491)	36	RLCA	10
		PLCA	17
		Postage and telephone	9
	36		36

Trial balance after adjustments

	Dr £	Cr £
Petty cash	20	
Capital		1,596
Drawings	1,435	
Sales		20,607
Purchases	15,486	
Purchases returns		210
Inventory at 1 January 20X4	2,107	
Fixtures and fittings	710	
Receivables ledger control account	1,829	
Payables ledger control account		2,061
Carriage on purchases	105	
Carriage on sales	188	
Rent and rates	460	
Light and heat	75	
Postage and telephone	100	
Sundry expenses	155	
Cash at bank	1,804	
	24,474	24,474

PRINCIPLES OF BOOKKEEPING CONTROLS

Test your understanding 5

Account name	Amount £	Dr ✓	Cr ✓
Rent	200	✓	
Motor expenses	200		✓

Account name	Amount £	Dr ✓	Cr ✓
Bank	1,600		✓
Suspense	1,600	✓	

Account name	Amount £	Dr ✓	Cr ✓
Discounts received	1,800		✓
Suspense	1,800	✓	

Account name	Amount £	Dr ✓	Cr ✓
Miscellaneous expenses	500	✓	
Suspense	500		✓

Account name	Amount £	Dr	Cr
VAT	100	✓	
Suspense	100		✓

Re-drafted trial balance

	£	£
Receivables	33,440	
Bank	1,200	
Sales		401,300
Inventory	24,300	
Wages	88,400	
Telephone	2,200	
Motor car	12,000	
VAT		5,200
Electricity	3,800	
Rent	16,400	
Purchases	241,180	
Purchases returns		1,600
Sales returns	4,200	
Office equipment	5,000	
Capital		49,160
Motor expenses	4,840	
Discounts allowed	4,010	
Discounts received		4,210
Payables		20,000
Drawings	40,000	
Miscellaneous expenses	500	
	481,470	481,470

PRINCIPLES OF BOOKKEEPING CONTROLS

Payroll procedures

Introduction

This chapter will consider one of the most significant payments that most businesses will make either weekly or monthly – wages and salaries.

ASSESSMENT CRITERIA
Produce journal entries to record bookkeeping transactions (3.1)

CONTENTS
1 Overview of the payroll function
2 Gross pay
3 Income tax
4 National Insurance/pension contributions
5 Other deductions
6 Payroll accounting procedures

1 Overview of the payroll function

1.1 Introduction

Payroll is one of the most important functions within a business. Payroll systems ensure that everyone is paid accurately and on time. The payroll staff have a responsibility to correctly calculate the amount of pay due to each employee and to ensure that both employees and external parties, such as HM Revenue and Customs (HMRC), are paid the correct amounts on time.

There are many elements of the payroll function and each will be briefly introduced in this section, and then considered in more detail later in the chapter.

1.2 Calculation of gross pay

The initial calculation to be carried out for each employee is the calculation of the employee's gross pay. Gross pay is the wage or salary due to the employee for work performed in the period. This calculation is performed weekly or monthly depending upon how frequently the employees are paid.

Gross pay may depend upon a number of factors, including:

- basic hours worked
- overtime hours worked
- bonus
- commission
- holiday pay
- sick pay.

1.3 Deductions

Once the gross pay for each employee has been determined then a number of items will be deducted to arrive at the net amount payable to the employee, known as the net pay.

Some deductions are compulsory or statutory:

- Income tax in the form of PAYE (Pay As You Earn).
- National Insurance Contributions (NIC) which can also be referred to as social security payments.

Other deductions are at the choice of the employer or employee and are therefore non-statutory, such as:

- Save as you earn (company savings scheme)
- Give as you earn (charitable donations)
- Union subscriptions
- Pension contributions.

1.4 Payment of wages or salaries

Once the net pay has been determined then each employee must be paid the correct amount on time.

1.5 Payments to external agencies

Employers deduct income tax and NIC from each employee's wages or salaries and then pay this to HMRC each month. At the same time, the employer must also pay its own employer's NIC contribution for each employee. Calculating and paying the employer's NIC is a further responsibility of the payroll function.

1.6 Accounting for wages and salaries

Once the wages and salaries for the period have been paid then the appropriate amounts must be correctly entered into the ledger accounts.

1.7 Accuracy and confidentiality

Whilst carrying out all of these calculations and functions it is important that the calculations are made with complete accuracy. Not only is the amount that each individual will be paid dependent upon these calculations but there is a statutory duty to make the correct deductions from gross pay and to pay these over to HMRC.

Payroll staff deal with confidential and sensitive information such as the rate of pay for an individual. It is of the utmost importance that such details are kept confidential and access by unauthorised personnel is prevented.

2 Gross pay

2.1 Introduction

Gross pay is the total amount earned by the employee before any deductions have been made. Gross pay can comprise many different elements, e.g.

- basic wages or salary
- overtime
- shift payments
- bonus
- commission
- holiday pay
- statutory sick pay (or SSP) and
- statutory maternity pay (or SMP).

2.2 Wages and salaries

Employees will have an agreed salary or monthly, weekly, or hourly rate.

Total earnings will need to be calculated for hourly-paid employees. The source of this information might be clock cards.

Definition

A clock card is a card that records the hours worked by an employee.

As the employee arrives or leaves, they put their card in the slot of a special clock-in/out machine. The mechanism inside the clock stamps the time on the card.

The payroll clerk would transfer the number of hours worked onto special calculation sheets.

2.3 Overtime and shift payments

Overtime and shift payments need to be identified so that the payroll clerk can calculate the amount payable to employees.

Overtime refers to any hours worked in excess of the agreed number of weekly or monthly hours for that employee. For example, it may be agreed that an employee has a standard working week of 38 hours. If they work for 42 hours in a week then they have worked 4 hours of overtime.

Overtime or shifts worked might be recorded on:

- clock cards
- time-sheets, or
- authorisation forms (signed by the employee's supervisor).

Some employees are paid at a higher rate for overtime. They might be paid at one and a half times the normal rate, which would be called time and a half.

Twice the normal rate is called double time.

Some employees might be paid premium rates or bonuses for working certain shifts.

2.4 Bonus and commission payments

The business may pay certain employees a bonus. This bonus may be for achieving a particular target, either for individuals or for teams,

Company directors often receive a bonus if the company achieves a certain level of profit.

Sales representatives may receive a commission as part of their salary. This commission is based on the value or volume of sales they make.

For instance, a sales representative might be paid a basic salary of £10,000 a year plus a 1% commission on the value of sales that they make.

2.5 Holiday pay

Most employers pay their employees even while they are on holiday.

If the employee is paid monthly, then there is no problem. The employee is paid the usual amount at the normal time.

If the employee is paid weekly, they may prefer to be paid for the holiday period in advance. This means that if the employee is taking two weeks' holiday they will have to be paid three weeks' wages at once.

2.6 Statutory sick pay (SSP) and statutory maternity pay (SMP)

In Principles of Bookkeeping Controls, the assessment will only expect knowledge of the treatments of basic wages and salaries, overtime and bonus payments.

If there is a reference to SSP or SMP, the task should make it clear as to how to deal with it.

3 Income tax

3.1 Introduction

Everybody in the UK has a potential liability to pay tax on his, her or their income.

Individuals pay **income tax**. The rate of income tax depends on the amount of the individual's income.

Definition

Income tax is a tax on individuals' income.

3.2 Tax-free income

Everybody is entitled to a personal allowance.

Definition

The personal allowance is the amount which an individual is allowed to earn without paying any tax.

3.3 How income tax is paid

Employees in the UK pay their income tax through the **PAYE** (or Pay As You Earn) **scheme**.

Definition

The PAYE scheme is a national scheme whereby employers deduct tax from their employees' wages and salaries when the employees are paid. The deductions are then paid monthly to HMRC by the employer.

PRINCIPLES OF BOOKKEEPING CONTROLS

The main advantages of this scheme from a tax perspective are:

- employees pay the tax as they earn the income
- most employees do not have to complete a tax return unless they have several different sources of income
- an advantage for HMRC is that employers act as unpaid tax collectors (this is a serious responsibility and employers can be fined for mistakes) and
- the government receives a steady stream of revenue throughout the year.

Test your understanding 1

Under the PAYE Scheme who pays over the income tax to HMRC?

A   The employee
B   The employer
C   The government
D   The Inspector of Taxes

4 National Insurance/pension contributions

4.1 What is National Insurance?

National Insurance is a state scheme which pays certain benefits including:

- retirement pensions
- widow's allowances and pensions
- jobseeker's allowance
- incapacity benefit, and
- maternity allowance.

The scheme is run by HMRC and funded by employees who are currently in employment.

Most people in employment (including partners in partnerships, and sole traders), who have earnings above a certain level, must pay National Insurance contributions.

4.2 Types of National Insurance contributions

Both the employer and the employee pay National Insurance contributions.

(a) **Employees' National Insurance contributions**

The employer deducts National Insurance contributions from an employee's weekly/monthly wage or salary, and pays the NI to HMRC on the employees' behalf. Income tax and National Insurance contributions are both taxes on income, but they have different historical origins and are calculated in different ways. Employees' National Insurance is now similar to income tax in many respects, and is really a form of income tax with another name.

Like income tax, employees' NI contributions are deducted from gross pay. The amount an employee pays is linked to his/her/their earnings, and is obtained by reference to National Insurance tables supplied by HMRC.

In Principles of Bookkeeping Controls, candidates are not required to know how to use NI tables.

(b) **Employer's National Insurance contributions**

In addition to deducting and repaying employees' National Insurance, an employer is required to pay the employer's National Insurance contributions for each employee to HMRC. The amount payable for each employee is linked to the size of the employee's earnings.

Employer's National Insurance contributions are therefore an employment tax. Employer's NI is not deducted from the employee's gross pay. They are an additional payroll cost to the employer, borne by the employer rather than the employee.

4.3 Pension contributions

Both the employer and the employee may contribute to a pension scheme.

(a) **Employees' pension contributions**

The employer deducts pension contributions from an employee's gross weekly wage or monthly salary, and pays these to the pension provider.

(b) **Employer's pension contributions**

Similar to the employer's national insurance contributions, the employer's pension contributions are an additional payroll cost to the employer, borne by the employer rather than the employee.

5 Other deductions

5.1 Deductions

The employee may also choose to have further deductions made from their gross pay. These include:

- **save as you earn scheme.** This is a strictly-governed scheme offered by some employers that allows the employee to save a regular amount each pay day. The agreed amount is deducted from gross pay, then this money is available to buy shares in the company at a later date.

- **give as you earn scheme**. This scheme allows employees to request that their employer withhold a certain amount from their salary each pay day then pay it over to a chosen charity on the employee's behalf.

- other payments. For example subscriptions to sports and social clubs and trade unions.

5.2 Summary of deductions and payments

Deductions: to process the payroll an employer must, for each employee, calculate:

- the gross earnings for the period
- the income tax (PAYE) payable out of these earnings
- the employee's NIC deductible
- the employer's NIC
- any non-statutory deductions
- net pay

Payments: the employer must then pay:

- the net pay to each employee
- all the non-statutory deductions to the appropriate organisation, e.g. union, pension company
- the employee's PAYE, the employee's NIC and the employer's NIC to HMRC for all employees.

Example 1

John earns £12,000 per annum. Details of John's pay for the month of May 20X4 are:

	£
PAYE	125
Employee's NIC	80
Employee contribution to personal pension scheme	50
Employer's NIC	85

Calculate:

(a) John's net pay

(b) the cost to the employer of employing John

(c) the amounts to be paid to the various organisations involved.

Solution

Calculation			Paid by employer to:
Gross pay per month		1,000	
Less: PAYE	125		HMRC
Employee's NIC	80		HMRC
Personal pension	50		Pension company
		(255)	
Net pay		745	John
Employer's NIC		85	HMRC

(a) John's net pay is £745.

(b) The cost of employing John is £1,085 (1,000 + 85).

(c) £50 is paid to the pension company.

£290 is paid to HMRC.

	£
PAYE	125
Employee's NIC	80
Employer's NIC	85
	290

Where there are many employees, the employer will pay the PAYE and NIC for all employees to HMRC with a single payment.

PRINCIPLES OF BOOKKEEPING CONTROLS

 Test your understanding 2

An employee has gross pay for a week of £368.70. The PAYE for the week is £46.45, the employer's NIC £30.97 and the employee's NIC £23.96.

What is the employee's net pay for the week?

6 Payroll accounting procedures

6.1 Introduction

The accounting for wages and salaries is based upon two fundamental principles:

- the accounts must reflect the full cost to the employer of employing the employee (which is their gross pay plus the employer's NI contribution)
- the accounts must show a liability for PAYE and NIC payable to HMRC on a regular basis, usually monthly.

Bookkeepers therefore need the following accounts:

(a) The wages expense account which shows the full cost of employing the employees.

(b) The HMRC liability account which shows the amount to be paid to HMRC.

(c) The wages and salaries control account which acts as a control over the entries in the accounts. There are different ways of using this control account, but AAT use it to control the gross pay and deductions from the employees, plus employer's NIC.

6.2 Accounting for payroll costs

The double entry reflects these two principles and uses the above accounts to process payroll.

1   Dr   Wages expense account
        Cr   Wages and salaries control account

    with the total expense to the business (gross pay plus employer's NIC)

2   Dr   Wages and salaries control account
        Cr   Bank account

    with the net wages paid to the employees

Payroll procedures: Chapter 4

3   Dr   Wages and salaries control account
         Cr   HMRC Liability

with those amounts payable to HMRC, both employee and employer contributions

4   Dr   Wages and salaries control account
         Cr   Other liability (e.g. pension, union)

with those amounts payable in respect of other deductions.

Example 2

The wages and salaries information for an organisation for a month is given as follows:

	£
Gross wages	34,000
PAYE deducted	7,400
NIC deducted	5,600
Net pay	21,000
Employer's NIC	7,800

Write up the relevant ledger accounts in the general ledger to reflect this.

Solution

Wages and salaries control account

		£		£
2	Bank account	21,000	1 Wages expense account (Gross pay)	34,000
3	HMRC Liability (PAYE)	7,400		
3	HMRC Liability (ees NIC)	5,600	1 Wages expense account (ers NIC)	7,800
3	HMRC Liability (ers NIC)	7,800		
		41,800		41,800

Wages expense account

	£		£
1 Wages and salaries control (Gross pay)	34,000		
1 Wages and salaries control (ers NIC)	7,800	Bal c/d	41,800
	41,800		41,800
Bal b/d	41,800		

PRINCIPLES OF BOOKKEEPING CONTROLS

HMRC liability

	£		£
		3 Wages and salaries control	7,400
		3 Wages and salaries control	5,600
Bal c/d	20,800	3 Wages and salaries control	7,800
	20,800		20,800
		Bal b/d	20,800

6.3 Commentary on the solution

(a) The wages and salaries control account monitors the payroll postings. The total gross pay is taken from the company payroll, as are the deductions for PAYE and NIC. Assuming that the company payroll schedule reconciles and no errors are made, the account should have a nil balance once all postings are complete.

(b) The wages expense account shows the total cost to the employer of employing the workforce (£41,800). This is the gross wages cost plus the employer's own NIC cost.

(c) The HMRC liability account shows the amount due to HMRC, i.e. PAYE + employee's and employer's NIC.

Test your understanding 3

Given below is a summary of an organisation's payroll details for a month.

	£
Gross wages	54,440
PAYE	11,840
Employees' NIC	8,960
Employer's NIC	12,480

You are required to prepare the journals to enter the figures in the general ledger accounts. Then state the balance on the control account, once the net amount has been paid to the employees.

Test your understanding 4

Steph earns £36,000 per annum. Steph's deductions for August 20X7 are:

	£
PAYE	530
Employee's NIC	275
Employer's pension contributions	100
Employee contribution to pension	100
Employer's NIC	350

Based on the information given, write up the wages expense, wages control, HMRC liability and pension liability accounts.

 Test your understanding 5

Maz pays employees by BACS every month and maintains a wages control account. A summary of last month's payroll transactions is shown below:

Item	£
Gross wages	35,000
Employer's NIC	4,200
Employees' NIC	2,970
Income tax	8,213
Employer pension	2,000
Employee pension	1,010

Record the journal entries needed in the general ledger to:

(i) Record the wages expense

(ii) Record the HMRC liability

(iii) Record the net wages paid to the employees

(iv) Record the pension liability.

Test your understanding 6

Given below is the wages book for the month of May 20X1 for a small business with four employees.

Wages book

Employee number	Gross pay £	PAYE £	Employee's NIC £	Employer's NIC £	Net pay £
001	1,200	151	78	101	971
002	1,400	176	91	118	1,133
003	900	113	58	76	729
004	1,550	195	101	130	1,254
	5,050	635	328	425	4,087

You are required to use the totals from the wages book to write up journal entries recording:

- the wages expense
- the HMRC liability
- the net wages paid to the employees.

You can then record these entries in the ledger accounts below.

Gross wages control account

	£		£

Wages expense account

		£		£
30 April	Balance b/d	23,446		

HM Revenue and Customs account

		£			£
19 May	CPB	760	30 April	Balance b/d	760

7 Summary

This chapter has introduced the taxation elements that affect the payment of wages and salaries. Candidates need to understand in principle how PAYE and NI works and be able to calculate the net pay to employees after deductions. Candidates need to understand how wages and salaries are accounted for in the general ledger. However, candidates do not need to be able to use HMRC tables.

PRINCIPLES OF BOOKKEEPING CONTROLS

Test your understanding answers

Test your understanding 1

B   The employer

Test your understanding 2

	£
Gross pay	368.70
Less: PAYE	(46.45)
NIC	(23.96)
Net pay	298.29

Test your understanding 3

1   Dr   Wages expense account

       Cr   Wages and salaries control account

with the total expense of £66,920

2   Dr   Wages and salaries control account

       Cr   HMRC liability account

with the PAYE of £11,840, and with the employee's NIC of £8,960 and with the employer's NIC of £12,480.

Once the net amount to be paid to the employee has been posted by debiting the wages and salaries control account and crediting the bank account with £33,640, the balance on the control account will be nil.

Test your understanding 4

Solution

Wages and salaries control account

	£		£
Bank account	2,095	Wages expense account	3,450
HMRC liability (PAYE + both NIC)	1,155		
Pension liability	200		
	3,450		3,450

Wages expense account

	£		£
Wages and salaries control (Gross + Er's NIC + Er's pension)	3,450	Bal c/d	3,450
	3,450		3,450

HMRC liability

	£		£
Bal c/d	1,155	Wages and salaries control	1,155
	1,155		1,155

Pension liability

	£		£
Bal c/d	200	Wages and salaries control	200
	200		200

PRINCIPLES OF BOOKKEEPING CONTROLS

Test your understanding 5

(i)

Account name	Amount £	Debit ✓	Credit ✓
Wages expense	41,200	✓	
Wages control	41,200		✓

(ii)

Account name	Amount £	Debit ✓	Credit ✓
Wages control	15,383	✓	
HMRC liability	15,383		✓

(iii)

Account name	Amount £	Debit ✓	Credit ✓
Wages control	22,807	✓	
Bank	22,807		✓

(iv)

Account name	Amount £	Debit ✓	Credit ✓
Wages control	3,010	✓	
Pension	3,010		✓

Test your understanding 6

Account name	Amount £	Dr ✓	Cr ✓
Wages expense	5,475	✓	
Wages control	5,475		✓

Account name	Amount £	Dr ✓	Cr ✓
HMRC liability	1,388		✓
Wages control	1,388	✓	

Account name	Amount £	Dr ✓	Cr ✓
Bank	4,087		✓
Wages control	4,087	✓	

Wages control

		£			£
31 May	Net pay: Bank	4,087	31 May	Gross: wages exp	5,050
	PAYE: HMRC	635	31 May	Ers NIC: wages exp	425
	Ees NIC: HMRC	328			
	Ers NIC: HMRC	425			
		5,475			5,475

Wages expense

		£			£
30 Apr	Balance b/d	23,446			
31 May	Gross: wages control	5,050			
	Ers NIC: control	425	31 May	Balance c/d	28,921
		28,921			28,921
31 May	Balance b/d	28,921			

HMRC liability

		£			£
19 May	CPB	760	30 Apr	Balance b/d	760
			31 May	PAYE: wages control	635
				Ees NIC: wages control	328
31 May	Balance c/d	1,388		Ers NIC: wages control	425
		2,148			2,148
			31 May	Balance b/d	1,388

PRINCIPLES OF BOOKKEEPING CONTROLS

The banking system and bank reconciliations

Introduction

This chapter will introduce the banking system. It will consider different forms of payment, how to ensure their validity and the effect different forms of payment have on an organisation's bank balance i.e. when banked funds are cleared and available for use.

Completion of this chapter will provide the knowledge to correctly prepare the cash book, compare the entries in the cash book to details on the bank statement and to prepare a bank reconciliation.

ASSESSMENT CRITERIA	CONTENTS
Payment methods (2.1)	1 Writing up the cash book
Use the bank statement to update the cash book (2.2)	2 The banking system
Complete bank reconciliation statements (2.3)	3 Preparing the bank reconciliation statement

1 Writing up the cash book

1.1 Introduction

Most businesses will have a separate cash receipts book and a cash payments book, which form part of the double-entry system. The closing cash balance is calculated from the opening balance at the beginning of the period, plus the receipts shown in the cash receipts book and minus the payments shown in the cash payments book for the period.

1.2 Balancing the cash book

To find the balance on the cash book when separate receipts and payments book are maintained, use the following calculation:

	£
Opening balance per the cash book	X
Add: Receipts in the period	X
Less: Payments in the period	(X)
Closing balance per the cash book	X

Example 1

The opening balance on the cash book was £358.72 on 1 June. During June, the cash payments book shows total payments made of £7,326.04 and the cash receipts book shows receipts of £8,132.76.

What is the closing balance on the cash book at the end of June?

Solution

		£
Opening balance at 1 June		358.72
Add:	Receipts for June	8,132.76
Less:	Payments for June	(7,326.04)
Balance at 30 June		1,165.44

PRINCIPLES OF BOOKKEEPING CONTROLS

Take care if the opening balance on the cash book is an overdraft balance. Any receipts in the period will reduce the overdraft and any payments will increase the overdraft.

Suppose that the opening balance on the cash book was £631.25 overdrawn on 1 June. During June, the cash payments book shows total payments made of £2,345.42 and the cash receipts book shows receipts of £1,276.45.

What is the closing balance on the cash book at the end of June?

Solution

	£
Opening balance at 1 June	(631.25)
Add: Receipts for June	1,276.45
Less: Payments for June	(2,345.42)
Balance at 30 June	(1,700.22)

Test your understanding 1

The opening balance at 1 January in a business's cash book was £673.42 overdrawn. During January, payments totalled £6,419.37 and receipts totalled £6,488.20.

What was the closing balance on the cash book at 31 January?

2 The banking system

2.1 The bank and customer relationship

The relationship between the bank and the customer is that of a receivable and payable.

If the bank holds money belonging to the customer, the money has to be repaid. Therefore from the bank's point of view, the customer is a payable (i.e. the bank owes money to the customer). From the customer's point of view, the bank account is a receivable (i.e. the customer is owed money by the bank).

However, when the customer borrows money from the bank the relationship is reversed. For the bank, the customer's outstanding loan is a receivable. For the customer, the amount owed to the bank is a payable.

This is also the case when the business has an overdraft with the bank. In this situation the business owes money to the bank.

2.2 Banking terminology

The debits and credits to cash/bank accounts in double-entry bookkeeping show:

- debits – money into the bank account
- credits – money out of the bank account.

On a bank statement, the terms are reversed as the statement is prepared from the bank's point of view.

When a customer has money in the bank account, this is described by the bank as a credit balance because the bank considers the balance to be a liability (a payable to the customer).

If the customer has an overdraft, then this is described by the bank as a debit balance, as the bank considers the balance as an asset (a receivable from the customer).

2.3 Banking services

People and businesses have bank accounts so they do not have to keep all their money as cash, which is subject to theft

There are three main types of bank account:

Current account	The current account is a business's normal working account. Cash and cheques received from customers are paid into this account. The business will be issued with a business account debit card for electronic payments and a cheque book so that expenses and suppliers can be paid by writing cheques.
	Current accounts are also the most common form of account for personal customers.
	Most banks, on request, will allow a business (or indeed a personal customer) an agreed level of overdraft. This means that when the current account does not have sufficient funds to cover payments made by the business, the bank will honour those payments up to the agreed overdraft limit. The bank will charge interest on any overdrawn balances and an arrangement fee for the setting up of the overdraft facility.

PRINCIPLES OF BOOKKEEPING CONTROLS

Deposit or savings accounts	A business can use a deposit account to hold short-term surplus funds because the interest earned is often considerably higher than that on current account balances. Money in deposit accounts can then be transferred to the current account when required. Some deposit accounts require a period of notice before funds can be transferred or removed from the account.
Loan accounts	An overdraft can be a useful method of short-term borrowing to fund the everyday expenses of a business, but if larger amounts are required (e.g. for the purchase of plant and machinery) then a separate loan should be taken out.
	A business loan can be offered to all types of business. Loans will normally be secured using the assets of the business. This means that the bank will have the rights to claim the assets of the business if the loan is not repaid. Alternatively, the personal guarantee of the owner of the business may be required.
	For the purchase of property, a commercial mortgage can be provided. The mortgage is normally for a long-term period (e.g. 25 years) and is secured on the property itself. Therefore if the mortgage is not repaid, the bank can sell the property in order to recover its money.

2.4 Cheques

 Definition

Cheque – An unconditional order in writing, signed by the drawer, requiring a bank to pay a certain sum of money on demand to a named person.

The parties involved in a cheque are:

- the drawer – the person writing the cheque.
- the payee – the person the cheque is to be paid to.
- the drawee – the bank upon whom the cheque is drawn, i.e. the bank that has issued the cheque book.

The banking system and bank reconciliations: **Chapter 5**

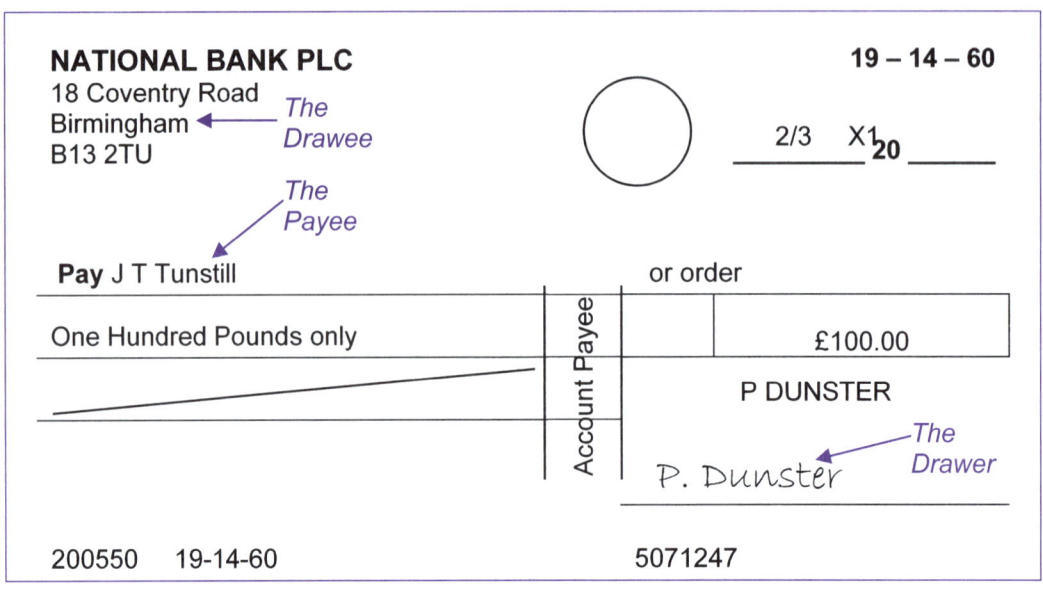

Test your understanding 2

The cheque shown below has been issued by Chang Fashions Limited. Give the name of:

(a) the drawer

(b) the drawee

(c) the payee.

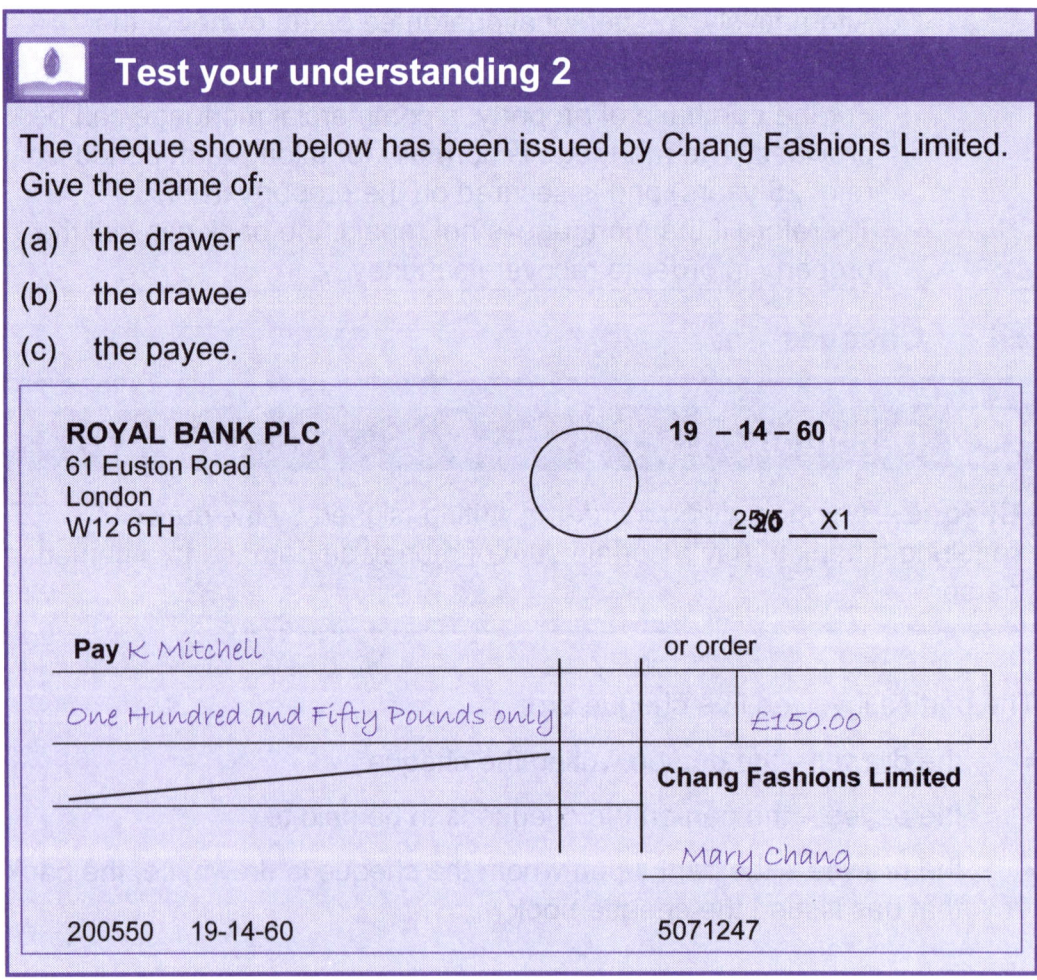

PRINCIPLES OF BOOKKEEPING CONTROLS

When a cheque has been paid in by a customer, the bank must carefully review that cheque before cashing it. Those checks include:

Date of the cheque	A cheque can become out of date as it is only valid for **six months** from the date of issue.
	A cheque which is dated later than the day on which it is written (known as a 'post-dated cheque') cannot be paid in until that later date. For example, a cheque written on 5 May 20X1 but dated 10 May 20X1 could not be paid into a bank account before 10 May 20X1.
	If a cheque is presented to the payee undated the payee can insert a date. The bank's cashier would normally ask the payee to do this. If any undated cheques are accidentally accepted by the bank, the bank's date stamp can be used to insert the date. Once a date is entered on a cheque it cannot, however, be altered by the payee.
Payee's name	The payee's name should be the same as the one shown on the account that the cheque is being paid into.
Words and figures	All relevant words and figures should be completed and agree. If an error is present, the cheque should be returned by the bank to the drawer for amendment or for a new cheque to be issued.
Signature	The cheque must be signed by the drawer.
Crossings	If the cheque has a crossing (two parallel lines on the face of the cheque), it must be paid into a bank account. It cannot be exchanged for cash over the counter. Pre-printed cheques carry crossings stating 'account payee only'. This means the cheque can only be paid into the account of the payee.

A customer has the right to stop a cheque right up until the bank pays it. The customer must write to the bank and give clear details of the payee's name, the cheque number and the amount payable.

> **Test your understanding 3**
>
> A cheque for £374 has been accepted by you in payment for a washing machine. As you record the cheque, you notice that it has been dated 1 June 20X2. Today's date is 1 June 20X3.
>
> (a) Will payment of the cheque by the drawer's bank be affected by the incorrect date?
>
> (b) Having noticed the error, is it acceptable for you to alter the cheque to the correct date?

2.5 How the clearing system works

The method by which the major banks process banked cheques is known as the clearing system..

The whole process of clearing cheques typically takes one working day.

The Cheque and Credit Clearing Company, which manages cheque-clearing in the UK, introduced the Image Clearing System in 2018. Banks and building societies can now process cheques as digital images, so cheques clear faster.

The process works as follows:

1   The payee pays the cheque into their bank

2   The payee's bank carries out security checks and then creates an image of the cheque (Note: some banks allow individuals to create the image using a mobile banking app or businesses using a cheque scanner)

3   The payee's bank sends the image securely through the image clearing system to the drawer's bank

4   The drawer's bank performs further security checks, ensuring that the cheque has not been paid before, and confirms that the drawer's account contains sufficient funds

5   The drawer's bank sends the money to the payee's bank which pays the funds into the payee's account.

Test your understanding 4

Fabien Cater has received a cheque for £1,000 from MEL Motor Factors Limited and has paid it into the bank. When asking if some cash can be drawn against the cheque, Fabien is told by the cashier that it is necessary to wait until the next week day after the cheque was paid in.

Explain briefly why the bank might ask Fabien to wait before cash can be drawn out against some or all of the £1,000.

2.6 Banker's drafts

 Definition

A **banker's draft**, sometimes referred to as a bank cheque, is a cheque issued by a bank rather than an individual. Funds are transferred from the individual's account to the bank. Then the bank issues the cheque, made payable to the payee requested by the individual.

Banker's drafts are often used for individuals making large purchases, such as cars, so that the payee does not need to wait for the cheque to clear. The fact that the banker's draft has been issued by the bank removes the risk to the payee of the cheque being returned or 'bouncing' due to insufficient funds in the drawer's account.

2.7 Building society cheques

 Definition

A **building society cheque** and bankers draft are similar. However, a building society cheque can be stopped by the drawer to prevent payment being made.

A building society can issue a cheque instead of cash when a withdrawal is made from an account. As with a banker's draft, the cheque is made payable to the payee requested by the account holder.

These cheques are written by the building society, knowing the cash is available.

2.8 Debit and credit cards

> **Definition**
>
> A **debit card** is a method of making payment direct from a bank account without having to write out a cheque. .

When a debit card is used to make a payment, the cardholder's bank account is automatically debited with the amount of the payment. The payment then appears on the customer's bank statement along with cheque payments, standing orders and direct debits.

> **Definition**
>
> **Credit cards** are issued by the credit card companies to allow customers to make purchases at certain shops, hotels, websites, etc. without using cash or cheques.

An individual opens an account with one of the credit card companies, completing and submitting an application form. If accepted, the individual will receive a credit card.

This credit card can then be used wherever that particular card is accepted.

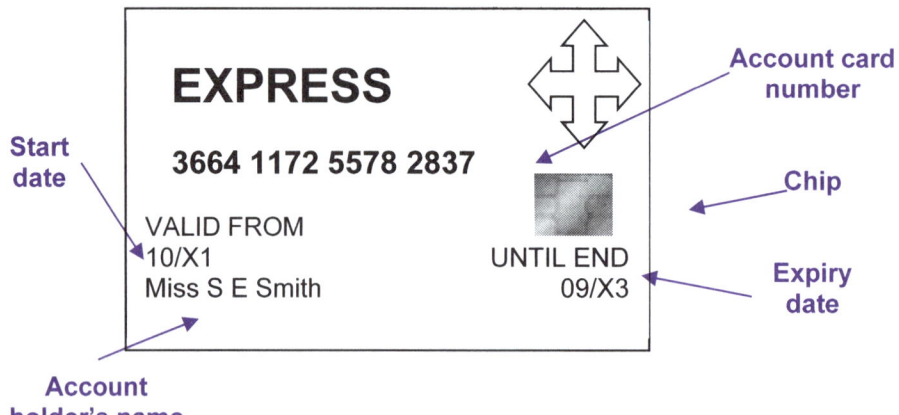

PRINCIPLES OF BOOKKEEPING CONTROLS

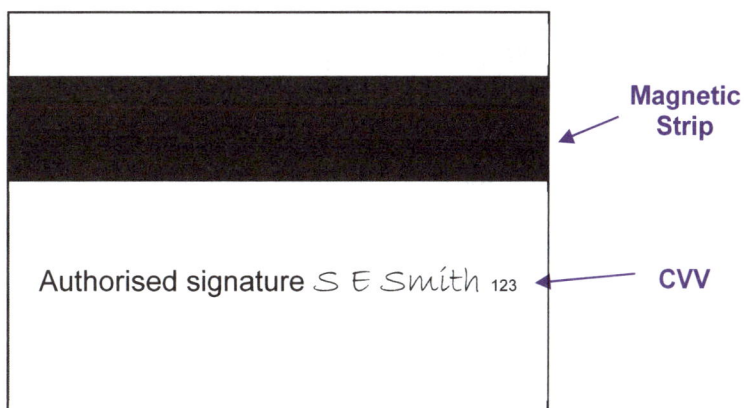

 Definition

CVV stands for **card verification value**. It is three or four digits on a card that adds an extra layer of security when making purchases online or over the phone. It provides verification that the user has a physical copy of the card in their possession and helps to protect account holders if the card number is stolen by identity thieves or hackers.

Each month the credit card holder receives a statement detailing the purchases for that month. The total amount is owed to the credit card company.

The cardholder has a choice of:

- paying a minimum balance, calculated by the credit card company dependent upon the amount owed
- paying off more than the minimum but less than the total balance outstanding
- paying off the total balance outstanding.

If the cardholder does not pay off the total balance within 25 days of receiving the statement, the cardholder will have to pay interest on the unpaid amount.

Businesses which make direct sales to the public are generally known as retailers. Retailers must have an agreement with the credit card company to be allowed to accept payment by that particular credit card.

In return for this service, the credit card company will normally charge the retailer a commission, usually a percentage, on each payment using that card.

Test your understanding 5

Which of the following details can NOT be determined from a customer's credit card (you can choose more than one answer).

	✓
The customer's name	
The customer's address	
The customer's credit card number	
The customer's credit limit	
The customer's credit card company	
The available amount the customer has to spend	

2.9 Standing orders and direct debits

A bank customer can transfer money from their account to another person's account by other methods which do not involve writing cheques. These are:

- standing orders
- direct debits.

Definition

A **standing order** (SO) is a customer's instruction to their bank to pay a fixed amount at regular intervals to a named party e.g. a monthly standing order to pay £600 rent to the landlord.

To arrange a standing order, the customer needs to sign a **standing order mandate** which authorises the bank to make the payments.

PRINCIPLES OF BOOKKEEPING CONTROLS

To FINANCIAL BANK PLC fb

_____ Branch   STANDING ORDER MANDATE

	Bank	Branch title (not address)	Sort code number
Please pay			
	Beneficiary's name		Account number
Credit			
	Amount in figures	Amount in words	
the sum of	£		
commencing	Date of first payment		Due date & frequency
	now/*	And thereafter every	
	Date and amount of last payment		
until		£	*until you receive further notice from me/us in writing
quoting the reference			and debit my/our account accordingly

Please cancel any previous standing order or direct debit in favour of the named beneficiary above

Special instructions

Account to be debited	Account number

Signature (s)   Date

* Delete if not applicable

Standing orders are ideal for paying regular bills such as insurance premiums. They can also be used to transfer money between a customer's different accounts, e.g. transferring surplus money each month from a current account into a deposit account.

> **Definition**
>
> A **direct debit** (DD) instruction allows authorised recipients to claim payments from a customer's bank account. These payments are covered by the direct debit guarantee to protect the customer.

Direct debits are better than standing orders when either

- the amount is uncertain or
- the date of payment is uncertain.

Direct debits are useful for paying items such as membership subscriptions which increase from year to year or monthly bills which alter in amount, such as credit card bills.

Both direct debits and standing orders continue to be valid until the customer cancels or changes them.

> **Test your understanding 6**
>
> Music World Limited needs to make regular monthly payments to Firmcare Finance Limited. The amount of the payment varies from month to month. Which service provided by the banks would appear to be the most appropriate?

2.10 BACS, CHAPS and Faster Payments

> **Definition**
>
> **BACS** (Bankers Automated Clearing System) – a method of clearing payments in which transactions are recorded on magnetic tape or disks (rather than on paper). Transactions are then processed at the BACS computer centre instead of through the clearing house. BACS can be used by companies which have been allowed to do so by the banks. BACS payments typically take up to 3 working days to clear.

BACS is used for:

- standing order payments
- direct debits
- salary payments.

PRINCIPLES OF BOOKKEEPING CONTROLS

Definition

A further service is also available to customers wishing to transfer large sums of money. This is **CHAPS** (Clearing House Automated Payments System).

Payments are credited to the payee on the same day as instructions are received. This is useful when a large sum of money needs to clear immediately, for example a property purchase.

Definition

FPS (Faster Payments Service) – an internet-based system introduced to reduce payment times between different banks' customer accounts. Transfer times can be reduced, from the three working days using BACS, to typically a few seconds.

Test your understanding 7

Indicate whether each of the following statements is true or false.

	True/False
When a cheque is banked the funds are available immediately	
A cheque has to be passed to the bank of the issuer before the money becomes available	
The clearing process is quicker for a building society than for a bank	
Cheques can only be processed by banks, not building societies	
Dishonoured cheques are returned to the drawer	
The drawer has the right to stop a cheque right up until the bank pays it	

3 Preparing the bank reconciliation statement

3.1 Introduction

At regular intervals, usually at least once a month, the cashier must check that the cash book is correct by comparing it to the bank statement.

3.2 Differences between the cash book and bank statement

The balance shown on the bank statement is unlikely to agree with the balance in the cash book for two main reasons.

(a) **Items in the cash book but not on the bank statement**

Certain items will have been entered in the cash book but will not appear on the bank statement at the time of the reconciliation.

Examples are:

- cheques received by the business and paid into the bank which have not yet appeared on the bank statement, due to the time lag of the clearing system. These are known as **outstanding or uncleared lodgements**.

- cheques issued by the business but which have not yet appeared on the bank statement, because the recipients have not yet paid them in, or the cheques are still in the clearing system. These are known as **unpresented cheques**.

- **errors** in the cash book (e.g. transposition of numbers, addition errors).

(b) **Items on the bank statement not in the cash book**

At the time of the bank reconciliation, items will appear on the bank statement that have not yet been entered into the cash book. These can occur due to the cashier not being aware of the existence of these items until receiving the bank statements. Examples are:

- **direct debit or standing order payments** that are on the bank statement but have not yet been entered in the cash payments book.

- **BACS or other receipts** paid directly into the bank account by a customer.

- **bank charges or bank interest** that the business is unaware of until the bank statement has been received.

- **errors** in the cash book discovered only when compared to the bank statement.
- **returned cheques** i.e. cheques from a customer paid in but then returned because the customer does not have sufficient funds in their bank to pay the cheque.

3.3 The bank reconciliation

Definition

Definition: A bank reconciliation is simply a statement that explains the differences between the balance in the cash book and the balance on the bank statement at a particular date.

A bank reconciliation is produced by following a standard set of steps.

1 Agree the opening balance on the bank statement and in the cash book.

➤ If the opening balance on the bank statement is not the same as the opening balance in the cash book, review the bank statement for the first few days to identify any prior-period reconciling items which have cleared. Tick these items on the bank statement to show they have been dealt with.

2 Agree that items on the bank statement appear in the cash book (tick off).

➤ Look at the descriptions and the amounts, as the descriptions may not match. Often the bank statement will simply show a cheque number, while the cash book will have the details of the customer or supplier name. Take care with receipts as the bank statement may show a number of receipts combined together into one.

➤ If there are items on the bank statement that do not appear in the cash book (e.g. bank charges), update the cash book. These updated items should then be ticked off.

3 Any unticked items in the cash book are reconciling items i.e. unpresented cheques or uncleared lodgements.

➤ These will need to be recorded as reconciling items in the bank reconciliation statement.

Bank reconciliation as at 31.7.20X9

	£
Balance as per bank statement	X
Less unpresented cheques	(X)
Add outstanding lodgements	X
Balance as per cash book	X

Deduct the unpresented cheques (cheques entered in the cash book but not yet appearing on the bank statement) because the bank balance will be reduced when they appear on the bank statement.

Add outstanding lodgements (cash receipts entered in the cash book but not yet appearing on the bank statement) because the bank balance will be increased when they appear on the bank statement.

It is also useful to remember that the bank reconciliation can be performed the opposite way round, as shown below:

Bank reconciliation as at 31.7.20X9

	£
Balance as per cash book	X
Add unpresented cheques	X
Less outstanding lodgements	(X)
Balance as per bank statement	X

When starting with the cash book balance, add back the unpresented cheques because the bank statement has not paid them out.

Deduct outstanding lodgements because the bank statement cleared the funds as received.

The cash book balance should then agree to the bank statement balance..

PRINCIPLES OF BOOKKEEPING CONTROLS

3.4 Debits and credits in bank statements

When comparing the cash book to the bank statement, it is easy to get confused with debits and credits. To understand the terminology, it is important to consider the entries separately from both the perspective of the business and the banks.

Business perspective

In the ledgers of a business, a debit represents an amount of money paid into the account and a credit represents an amount of money paid out of the account.

This is because the cash book represents an asset for the business.

When a business account is overdrawn, the business will owe the bank money. The cash book will show a credit balance as the business has a liability.

Banks perspective

From the bank's perspective, the situation is reversed. On the bank statement, a credit represents an amount of money paid into the account and a debit represents an amount of money paid out of the account.

From the bank's viewpoint, the account is a payable (a liability).

For the bank, an overdraft represents an asset (the business will owe the bank money) and is therefore a debit balance.

Example 2

On 30 April, Tomasso's received the following bank statement as at 28 April 20X2.

Today's date is 30 April 20X2.

QC Bank
QC Street, London
To: Tomasso's   Account No 92836152   30 April 20X2

Date	Details	Debit	Credit	Balance
20X2		£	£	£
2 April	Bal b/f			100 C
3 April	Cheque 101	55		45 C
4 April	Cheque 103	76		31 D
6 April	Bank Giro Credit		1,000	969 C
9 April	Cheque 105	43		926 C
10 April	Cheque 106	12		914 C
11 April	Cheque 107	98		816 C
21 April	Direct Debit RBC	100		716 C
22 April	Direct Debit OPO	150		566 C
23 April	Interest received		30	596 C
24 April	Bank charges	10		586 C
28 April	Bank Giro Credit DJA		250	836 C

The cash book at 28 April 20X2 is shown below.

Date 20X2	Details	Bank £	Date 20X2	Chq No	Details	Bank £
	Balance b/f	100	1 April	101	Alan & Co	55
06 April	Prance Dance Co.	1,000	2 April	102	Amber's	99
23 April	Interest received	30	2 April	103	Kiki & Co	76
23 April	Graham Interiors	2,000	5 April	104	Marta	140
25 April	Italia Design	900	6 April	105	Nina Ltd	43
			7 April	106	Willy Wink	12
			8 April	107	Xylophones	98

The opening balance is £100 per both the bank statement and the cash book. So no opening reconciliation is necessary.

PRINCIPLES OF BOOKKEEPING CONTROLS

Then tick off the items in the bank statement to the cash book, as shown below:

Date	Details	Debit £	Credit £	Balance £
2 April	Bal b/f			100 C
3 April	Cheque 101	✓55		45 C
4 April	Cheque 103	✓76		31 D
6 April	Bank Giro Credit		✓1,000	969 C
9 April	Cheque 105	✓43		926 C
10 April	Cheque 106	✓12		914 C
11 April	Cheque 107	✓98		816 C
21 April	Direct Debit RBC	100		716 C
22 April	Direct Debit OPO	150		566 C
23 April	Interest received		✓30	596 C
24 April	Bank charges	10		586 C
28 April	Bank Giro Credit DJA		250	836 C

This leaves 4 unticked items. The cash book is then updated as below.

Date 20X2	Details	Bank £	Date 20X2	Chq No	Details	Bank £
	Balance b/d	100	1 April	101	Alan & Co	✓55
06 April	Prance Dance Co.	✓1,000	2 April	102	Amber's	99
23 April	Interest received	✓30	2 April	103	Kiki & Co	✓76
23 April	Graham Interiors	2,000	5 April	104	Marta	140
25 April	Italia Design	900	6 April	105	Nina Ltd	✓43
28 April	DJA	250	7 April	106	Willy Wink	✓12
			08 April	107	Xylophones	✓98
			21 April	–	DD – RBC	100
			22 April	–	DD – OPO	150
			24 April	–	Bank charges	10
			28 April	–	Balance c/d	3,497
		4,280				4,280
29 April	Balance b/d	3,497				

Once the cash book has been updated, there are 4 remaining unticked items.

These are the items that will be entered onto the bank reconciliation, as shown below:

Bank reconciliation statement as at 28 April 20X2	£
Balance per bank statement	836
Add:	
Name: Graham's Interior	2,000
Name: Italia Design	900
Total to add	2,900
Less:	
Name: Amber's	99
Name: Marta	140
Total to subtract	239
Balance as per cash book	3,497

3.5 Opening balances disagree

When producing the bank reconciliation, it is important to take any differences between the opening cash book and the opening bank statement balances into account.

The balances on the bank statement and in the cash book do not agree at the start of the period for the same reasons that they do not agree at the end, i.e. unpresented cheques and uncleared lodgements.

Example 3

The bank statement and cash book of Jones for the month of December 20X8 start as follows.

		Bank statement		
		Debit £	Credit £	Balance £
1 Dec 20X8	Balance b/d			8,570C
2 Dec 20X8	0073	125		8,445C
2 Dec 20X8	0074	130		8,315C
3 Dec 20X8	Sundries		105	8,420C

PRINCIPLES OF BOOKKEEPING CONTROLS

Cash book

	£		£
1 Dec 20X8 b/d	8,420	Cheque 0075 Wages	200
Sales	320	Cheque 0076 Rent	500

Required:

Explain the difference between the opening balances.

Solution

The difference in the opening balance is as follows.

£8,570 – £8,420 = £150

This difference is due to the following:

	£
Cheque 0073	125
Cheque 0074	130
	–––––
	255
Sundry credit 3 Dec 20X8	(105)
	–––––
	150
	–––––

These items would have been in the cash book in November but only appear on the bank statement in December. The items would have been included in November's reconciliation. The brought forward reconciling items will therefore be matched and ticked against the entries in the November cash book. The December reconciliation will then proceed as normal.

The banking system and bank reconciliations: **Chapter 5**

 Test your understanding 8

Below is a bank statement for Alpha Ltd at 31 May 20X2.

Bark Lays Bank plc
High Street, London SE8 1ND
To: Alpha Ltd   Account No 48774900   31 May 20X2

Date	Details	Debit	Credit	Balance
20X2		£	£	£
1 May	Bal b/d			886 D
3 May	Cheque no 0041	2,000		2,886 D
6 May	Bank Giro Credit		360	2,526 D
7 May	Cheque no 0043	840		3,366 D
10 May	BACS		6,200	2,834 C
10 May	Credit		630	3,464 C
10 May	Credit		880	4,344 C
25 May	Bank Interest		40	4,384 C
31 May	BACS		460	4,844 C
		D = Debit	C= Credit	

Alpha's cash book for the month of May is shown below.

Date 20X2	Details	Bank £	Date 20X2	Chq No	Details	Bank £
			1 May		Balance b/d	526
6 May	Shaws	630	3 May	0041	Bills Farm	2,000
6 May	Andrew Ltd	880	3 May	0042	Cows Head	3,240
			5 May	0043	Adam Ant	840
			30 May	0044	Miles to Go	700

Update Alpha's cash book.

3.6 Returned cheques

A customer may send a cheque in payment of an invoice without having sufficient funds in the account with Bank A.

The business receives the cheque and pays into its account with Bank B and the cheque will go into the clearing system. Bank B will credit our account with the funds in anticipation of the cheque being honoured.

Bank A however will not pay funds into our account with Bank B. Bank B will then remove the funds from the business's account.

PRINCIPLES OF BOOKKEEPING CONTROLS

The net effect is that on the business bank statement, the cheque will appear as having been paid in (a credit on the bank statement), and then will appear later as paid out (a debit on the bank statement).

The original credit on the bank statement will appear in the business cashbook as a debit in the normal way. However, the debit on the bank statement (the return of the cheque) will not be in the cash book. The business will have to credit the cash book as effectively money is paid out.

These cheques are technically referred to as 'returned cheques', 'dishonoured cheques' or 'bounced cheques'.

Example 4

C sends a cheque to S in payment of an invoice for £300.

(a) S will enter this cheque into its accounts as follows:

Cash book

	£		£
RLCA	300		

RLCA

	£		£
		Cash book	300

The cheque will appear on S's bank statement as a credit entry.

(b) When the cheque is dishonoured, S will enter this cheque into its accounts as follows:

Cash book

	£		£
		RLCA	300

RLCA

	£		£
Cash book	300		

The journal entry will be

Dr   RLCA   300
Cr   Cash book   300

This entry reinstates the receivable, showing that C still owes S £300.

The dishonoured cheque will appear on the bank statement as a debit entry.

The banking system and bank reconciliations: **Chapter 5**

Test your understanding 9

Given below is the cash book of a business and the bank statement for the week ending 20 April 20X1.

Required:

Compare the cash book to the bank statement and note any differences that you find.

Cash book

April		£	April		£
16	Donald & Co	225.47	16	Balance b/d	310.45
17	Harper Ltd	305.68	17	Cheque 03621	204.56
17	Fisler Partners	104.67	18	Cheque 03622	150.46
18	Denver Ltd	279.57	19	Cheque 03623	100.80
19	Gerald Bros	310.45	19	Cheque 03624	158.67
20	Johnson & Co	97.68	20	Cheque 03625	224.67
			20	Balance c/d	173.91
		1,323.52			1,323.52

EXPRESS BANK   CONFIDENTIAL

High Street   Account   CURRENT   Sheet no. 0213
Fenbury
TL4 6JY   Account name P L DERBY LTD
Telephone: 01693 422130

Statement date 20 April 20X1   Account Number 40429107

Date April	Details	Withdrawals (£)	Deposits (£)	Balance (£)
16	Balance from sheet 0212			310.45 OD
17	DD – District Council	183.60		494.05 OD
18	Credit		225.47	
19	Credit		104.67	
	Cheque 03621	240.56		
	Bank interest	3.64		408.11 OD
20	Credit		305.68	
	Credit		279.57	
	Cheque 03622	150.46		
	Cheque 03624	158.67		131.99 OD

| DD | Standing order | DD | Direct debit | CP | Card purchase |
| AC | Automated cash | OD | Overdrawn | TR | Transfer |

PRINCIPLES OF BOOKKEEPING CONTROLS

Test your understanding 10

Graham

The cash account of Graham showed a debit balance of £204 on 31 March 20X3. A comparison with the bank statements revealed the following:

			£
1	Cheques drawn but not presented		3,168
2	Amounts paid into the bank but not credited		723
3	Entries in the bank statements not recorded in the cash account		
	(i)	Standing orders	35
	(ii)	Interest credited	18
	(iii)	Bank charges	14
4	Balance on the bank statement at 31 March 20X3		2,618

Tasks

(a) Show the appropriate adjustments required in the cash account of Graham bringing down the correct balance at 31 March 20X3.

(b) Prepare a bank reconciliation statement at that date.

Test your understanding 11

The following are the cash book and bank statements of KT Ltd.

Receipts June 20X1

CASH BOOK – JUNE 20X1				
Date	Details	Total	Receivables ledger control	Other
1 June	Balance b/d	7,100.45		
8 June	Cash and cheques	3,200.25	3,200.25	–
15 June	Cash and cheques	4,100.75	4,100.75	–
23 June	Cash and cheques	2,900.30	2,900.30	–
30 June	Cash and cheques	6,910.25	6,910.25	–
		£24,212.00	£17,111.55	

The banking system and bank reconciliations: Chapter 5

Payments June 20X1

Date June	Payee	Chq no	Total £	Payables ledger control £	Operating overhead £	Admin overhead £	Other £
1	Hawsker Chemical	116	6,212.00	6,212.00			
7	Wales Supplies	117	3,100.00	3,100.00			
15	Wages and salaries	118	2,500.00		1,250.00	1,250.00	
16	Drawings	119	1,500.00				1,500.00
18	Blyth Chemical	120	5,150.00	5,150.00			
25	Whitby Cleaning Machines	121	538.00	538.00			
28	York Chemicals	122	212.00	212.00			
			19,212.00	15,212.00	1,250.00	1,250.00	1,500.00

Bank statement

Crescent Bank plc
High Street
Sheffield
Account: Alison Robb t/a KT Ltd
Account no: 57246661

Statement no: 721
Page 1

Date	Details	Payments £	Receipts £	Balance £
20X1				
1 June	Balance b/d			8,456.45
1 June	113	115.00		8,341.45
1 June	114	591.00		7,750.45
1 June	115	650.00		7,100.45
4 June	116	6,212.00		888.45
8 June	CC		3,200.25	4,088.70
11 June	117	3,100.00		988.70
15 June	CC		4,100.75	5,089.45
15 June	118	2,500.00		2,589.45
16 June	119	1,500.00		1,089.45
23 June	120	5,150.00		4,060.55 O/D
23 June	CC		2,900.30	1,160.25 O/D

Key:	S/O	Standing Order	DD	Direct Debit
	CC	Cash and cheques	CHGS	Charges
	BACS	Bankers automated clearing	O/D	Overdrawn

PRINCIPLES OF BOOKKEEPING CONTROLS

Task

Examine the business cash book and the business bank statement shown in the data provided above. Prepare a bank reconciliation statement as at 30 June 20X1. Set out your reconciliation in the pro-forma below.

Proforma

BANK RECONCILIATION STATEMENT AS AT 30 JUNE 20X1

£

Balance per bank statement
Outstanding lodgements:

Unpresented cheques:

_____

Balance per cash book   £

_____

4 Summary

This chapter has introduced the details of the UK banking system. In particular, awareness of how the clearing system works, of the different methods of payment through the banking system and how credit and debit cards work

Candidates will need to understand what makes a valid cheque and be able to identify a cheque that is not valid.

The chapter explored the concept of the bank reconciliation and produced some examples, after producing an updated cash book..

Test your understanding answers

Test your understanding 1

	£
Opening balance	(673.42)
Payments	(6,419.37)
Receipts	6,488.20
Closing balance	(604.59)

The closing balance is £604.59 overdrawn.

Test your understanding 2

(a) Mary Chang, on behalf of Chang Fashions Limited.

(b) Royal Bank plc.

(c) K Mitchell.

Test your understanding 3

(a) Yes. The cheque is out of date and must be re-issued by the drawer.

(b) No.

Test your understanding 4

The cheque must pass through the clearing system before the bank knows whether or not it has been paid. In the meantime, the bank may be reluctant to allow Fabien to draw out cash against uncleared funds.

PRINCIPLES OF BOOKKEEPING CONTROLS

Test your understanding 5

	✓
The customer's name	
The customer's address	✓
The customer's credit card number	
The customer's credit limit	✓
The customer's credit card company	
The available amount the customer has to spend	✓

Test your understanding 6

Direct debit. Standing order is not appropriate since the amount of the payment varies from month to month.

Test your understanding 7

	True/False
When a cheque is banked the funds are available immediately Explanation – Cheques need to go through a clearing process with funds normally available after 3 days	FALSE
A cheque has to be passed to the bank of the issuer before the money becomes available	TRUE
The clearing process is quicker for a building society than for a bank Explanation – The clearing process is either the same length of time or longer for building societies than for banks	FALSE
Cheques can only be processed by banks, not building societies Explanation – Building societies also offer banking services and so can process cheques	FALSE
Dishonoured cheques are returned to the drawer Explanation – Dishonoured cheques are returned to the payee.	FALSE
The drawer has the right to stop a cheque right up until the banker pays it	TRUE

Test your understanding 8

Updated cash book:

Date	Details	£	Date	Chq	Details	£
			1 May		Balance b/d	526
6 May	Shaws	630	3 May	0041	Bills Farm	2,000
6 May	Andrew Ltd	880	3 May	0042	Cows Head	3,240
10 May	BACS	6,200	5 May	0043	Adam Ant	840
25 May	Bank Interest	40	30 May	0044	Miles to Go	700
31 May	BACS	460				
			31 May		Balance c/d	904
		8,210				8,210
1 June	Balance b/d	904				

Test your understanding 9

Cash book

April		£	April		£
16	Donald & Co	225.47✓	16	Balance b/d	310.45✓
17	Harper Ltd	305.68✓	17	Cheque 03621	204.56
17	Fisler Partners	104.67✓	18	Cheque 03622	150.46✓
18	Denver Ltd	279.57✓	19	Cheque 03623	100.80
19	Gerald Bros	310.45	19	Cheque 03624	158.67✓
20	Johnson & Co	97.68	20	Cheque 03625	224.67
			20	Balance c/d	173.91
		1,323.52			1,323.52

There are three unticked items on the bank statement:

- direct debit £183.60 to the District Council

- cheque number 03621 £240.56 – this has been entered into the cash book as £204.56

- bank interest £3.64.

Cheques 03623 and 03625 are unticked items in the cash book but these are payments that have not yet cleared through the banking system. Also, the receipts from Gerald Bros and Johnson & Co have not yet cleared the banking system.

PRINCIPLES OF BOOKKEEPING CONTROLS

EXPRESS BANK CONFIDENTIAL

Date	Details	Withdrawals (£)	Deposits (£)	Balance (£)
April				
16	Balance from sheet 0212			310.45 OD
17	DD – District Council	183.60		494.05 OD
18	Credit		225.47 ✓	
19	Credit		104.67 ✓	
	Cheque 03621	240.56		
	Bank interest	3.64		408.11 OD
20	Credit		305.68 ✓	
	Credit		279.57 ✓	
	Cheque 03622	150.46 ✓		
	Cheque 03624	158.67 ✓		131.99 OD

| DD | Standing order | DD | Direct debit | CP | Card purchase |
| AC | Automated cash | OD | Overdrawn | TR | Transfer |

Test your understanding 10

(a)

Cash account

	£		£
Balance b/d	204		
Interest received	18	Standing orders	35
		Bank charges	14
		Balance c/d	173
	222		222
Balance b/d	173		

(b)

BANK RECONCILIATION STATEMENT AT 31 MARCH 20X3

	£
Balance per bank statement	2,618
Add: Outstanding lodgements	723
	3,341
Less: Unpresented cheques	(3,168)
Balance per cash account	173

Test your understanding 11

BANK RECONCILIATION STATEMENT AS AT 30 JUNE 20X1

	£	£
Balance per bank statement		(1,160.25) O/D
Outstanding lodgements: 30 June 20X1		6,910.25
		5,750.00
Unpresented cheques:		
121	538.00	
122	212.00	
		(750.00)
Balance per cash book below		£5,000.00
Cash book June 20X1:		
Opening balance 1 June		7,100.45
Cash received: June		17,111.55
Cash paid: June		(19,212.00)
Balance per cash book 30 June 20X1		£5,000.00

MOCK ASSESSMENT

PRINCIPLES OF BOOKKEEPING CONTROLS

1 Mock Assessment Questions

Task 1 (10 marks)

This task is about using control accounts.

This task contains parts (a) to (c).

A receivables ledger control account balance is shown in the general ledger.

(a) Identify which ONE of the following is correct in relation to the receivables ledger control account. **(1 mark)**

	✓
A receivables ledger control account should always be produced by the same person who produces the subsidiary ledgers as this improves accuracy.	
A receivables ledger control account enables discrepancies between the bank and the subsidiary ledger to be quickly identified.	
A receivables ledger control account enables quick identification of the total amount owed to the business by customers.	
A receivables ledger control account enables quick identification of an amount owed by a particular customer.	

You work in the accounts department of Maskco Ltd. Your manager has run a report which shows a credit balance on the VAT control account at the end of May of £6,500. The credit balance at the end of April was £4,650. Your manager has asked you to prepare a VAT control account to explain why May shows a higher balance.

Mock Assessment Questions

The following information has been recorded for the month of May:

Item	£
VAT on purchases	6,927
VAT on purchases returns	96
VAT on sales	10,760
VAT on sales returns	156
VAT on discounts allowed	24
VAT on discounts received	36
VAT on cash sales	3,180
Payment made to HMRC	5,115

(b) Complete the VAT control account below for May by selecting an entry from each pick list and entering amounts in the spaces provided. (8 marks)

VAT Control Account

Details	Amount £	Details	Amount £
		Balance b/d	4,650
Balance c/d	6,500		

Select your account names from the following list: Purchases, Purchases returns, Sales, Sales returns, Discounts allowed, Discounts received, Bank, Cash sales

PRINCIPLES OF BOOKKEEPING CONTROLS

Vocid Ltd has the following payables ledger control account:

Payables ledger control account

Details	Amount £	Details	Amount £
Purchases returns	1,230	Balance b/d	13,452
Bank	33,692	Purchases	53,478
Discounts received	420		
Balance c/d			

(c) What will be the balance carried down on the payables ledger control account? **(1 mark)**

£ ☐

Task 2 (10 marks)

This task is about reconciling control accounts.

This task contains tasks (a) to (c)

The balance on the payables ledger control account will appear in the year-end trial balance. It is important to reconcile this to the payables ledger.

(a) **Identify which ONE of the following statements is a reason for completing this reconciliation.** **(1 mark)**

	✓
Any errors identified can be identified and included in the suspense account balance to investigate and resolve.	
The payables ledger can be deleted once it has been reconciled which helps to keep record keeping simple.	
Errors in either the payables ledger control account or the payables ledger can be identified and corrected.	
The payables ledger control account is always more accurate than the payables ledger.	

Mock Assessment Questions

You work in the accounts department of Dolt Ltd. Your manager has asked you to reconcile the balance on the receivables ledger account with the customer report of receivables ledger account balances. Your manager provided the following report dated 31 August:

Customer name	Agreed credit period	Account Ref	£
Building Trades Ltd			27,432
Easy Construction Ltd			11,096
Simplebuild Ltd			12,670
Roofit Ltd			715
Fixit Plumbers			245
Bespoke Tables Ltd			306
Joiner Brothers			8,130
Shockwave Electricians			1,515

(b) (i) If the receivables ledger control balance reconciles with the receivables ledger, what will be the balance? **(2 marks)**

£ 62,109

The balance on the receivables ledger control account is £62,380.

(b) (ii) Complete the following statement **(2 marks)**

The receivables ledger is

| £ 271 | Higher/lower* | (* delete which does not apply) |

than the receivables ledger control account.

PRINCIPLES OF BOOKKEEPING CONTROLS

The payables ledger control account shows a balance of £76,532 but the individual balances in the payables ledger total £75,842.

(c) Identify whether each of the following may explain differences between the two balances (5 marks)

Reason	May explain the difference	Does not explain the difference
An individual ledger account balance was included twice in the total of payables ledger account balances.		
Early settlement discount received was omitted from the payables ledger control account.		
A cash purchase has not been recorded in the accounting records.		
An individual ledger account balance was omitted from the list of payables ledger account balances.		
A transposition error was made when recording a purchase in the purchases daybook.		

Task 3 (8 marks)

This task is about payment methods and reconciling the cash book to the bank statement.

This task contains tasks (a) to (c)

(a) Insert ONE payment method for each description into the space provided. (4 marks)

A plastic card issued by a bank that permits the account holder to purchase goods on credit.	
An electronic system used to make payments from one bank account to another, mainly used for direct debits and credits, with transfers normally taking up to three working days.	
A regular payment of the same amount that is paid on a specified date.	
A plastic card issued by a bank allowing the account holder to transfer money electronically from their bank account when making a purchase of goods.	

Mock Assessment Questions

Select your payment method from the following list: BACS, Cash, CHAPS, Cheque, Credit card, Debit Card, Direct debit, Standing order

(b) Identify which ONE of the following statements is true (1 mark)

	✓
The balance on the bank statement will always be the same as the cash book balance.	
An overdrawn balance of £750 on the bank statement would be equivalent to a credit balance of £750 in the cash book.	
There are never errors in the transactions recorded on the bank statement.	

(c) Identify whether each of the following statements is true or false (3 marks)

Statement	True	False
Transactions which are not yet recorded in the cash book are examples of timing differences.		
Comparing the debit side of the cash book to the amounts paid in per the bank statement will enable any automated receipts that have been missed in the cash book to be identified		
The cash book should not include payments made by direct debit or standing order.		

PRINCIPLES OF BOOKKEEPING CONTROLS

Task 4 (12 marks)

This task is about reconciling a bank statement with the cash book.

The cash book for Kim's clothing business at 30 June is shown below. Kim pays all suppliers by cheque and all customers pay Kim by cheque or bank transfer.

Update the cash book, calculate the closing balance and prepare a bank reconciliation at 30 June. (12 marks)

Dragon Bank plc

230 Dentist Row, Northwood, NO7 8YT

To: Kim Adams   Account No 82730193   30 June 20X7

Statement of account

Date 20X7	Detail	Paid out £	Paid in £	Balance £	
06 Jun	Balance b/f			12,000	C
06 Jun	Cheque 11231	2,131		9,869	C
06 Jun	Cheque 11232	123		9,746	C
07 Jun	Cheque 11233	892		8,854	C
07 Jun	Cheque 11234	2,141		6,713	C
07 Jun	Bank Giro Credit Wright Bro's		1,532	8,245	C
12 Jun	Cheque 11235	212		8,033	C
14 Jun	Direct Debit Pink Panther	531		7,502	C
20 Jun	Direct Debit Aldo Insurers	900		6,602	C
21 Jun	Bank charges	20		6,582	C
22 Jun	Overdraft fee	15		6,567	C
24 Jun	Paid in at Dragon Bank		300	6,867	C

D = Debit C = Credit

Mock Assessment Questions

Cash book

Date 20X7	Details	Bank £	Date 20X7	Chq No	Details	Bank £
1 June	Balance b/f	12,000	2 June	11231	Ally & Co	2,131
22 June	A Dude	300	2 June	11232	Mr Wong	123
23 June	XPT Ltd	1,500	2 June	11233	Nina's Supplies	892
23 June	Marks Bros	2,150	2 June	11234	Bits & Bobs	2,141
			8 June	11235	PPP Ltd	212
			18 June	11236	Mama's Materials	2,350
			20 June	–	Aldo Insurers	900
			22 June	11237	George Richards	5,000

Select your entries for the 'Details' column from the following list: A Dude, Aldo Insurers, Ally & Co, Balance b/d, Balance c/d, Bank charges, Closing balance, George Richards, Bits & Bobs, Mama's Materials, Marks Brothers, Mr Wong, Nina's Supplies, Opening balance, Overdraft fees, Pink Panther, PPP Ltd, Wright Bros, XPT Ltd

PRINCIPLES OF BOOKKEEPING CONTROLS

Bank reconciliation statement	£
Balance per bank statement	6,867
Outstanding lodgements	
Total outstanding lodgements	
Unpresented cheques	
Total unpresented cheques	
Balance as per cash book	

Select your entries for the 'Details' column from the following list: A Dude, Aldo Insurers, Ally & Co, Balance b/d, Balance c/d, Bank charges, Closing balance, George Richards, Bits & Bobs, Mama's Materials, Marks Brothers, Mr Wong, Nina's Supplies, Opening balance, Overdraft fees, Pink Panther, PPP Ltd, Wright Bros, XPT Ltd

Task 5 (10 marks)

This task is about using the journal.

This task contains tasks (a) to (c)

(a) **Identify which TWO of the following situations would be a correct use of the journal.** (2 marks)

	✓
Akira identified that a credit sale transaction was recorded twice in the sales day book. Akira will correct this by recording the adjustment in the journal.	
Bao paid for some office cleaning materials from petty cash and has recorded this transaction in the journal.	
Nimay wanted to record a contra between the payables ledger control account and the receivables ledger control account. Nimay recorded this transaction in the journal.	
Amory recorded prompt payment discount received from a supplier in the journal.	

Mock Assessment Questions

A journal was recorded in the accounting system as follows:

Journal Number 46		Date: 30 November	
Account name	**Debit £**	**Credit £**	**Description**
Payroll liabilities: employees		25,434	Net pay
Payroll expenses - wages	31,763		Gross pay
Payroll expenses - taxes	2,570		National insurance - employer
Payroll liabilities - HMRC		3,028	National insurance - employee
Payroll liabilities - HMRC		2,570	National Insurance - employer
Payroll liabilities - HMRC		3,301	PAYE

Prior to this journal, the balance on the Payroll liabilities - HMRC account was a credit balance of £128

(b) After the journals are processed, what will be the revised balance on the Payroll Liabilities - HMRC account? (2 marks)

£ ☐

PRINCIPLES OF BOOKKEEPING CONTROLS

The following invoice has been outstanding for over six months and Alex wishes to write the amount off as an irrecoverable debt.

Sales invoice

Car Spares Ltd
123 Acacia Avenue
Barking BA7 2EQ
VAT registration 446 4482 01
Invoice number 54879

To: Theresa Green
26 Daneville Road
Colchester CO2 HO2
15 May 20XX

	£
1 Piston crown, skirt and pin @ £437.50	437.50
VAT @ 20%	87.50
Total	525.00

Terms: Net monthly account

(c) Complete the journal entries below to record the irrecoverable debt write off in the general ledger. You should select the account name from the picklist and then include the appropriate amount in either the Debit or Credit column of the journal entry.

(6 marks)

Account name	Amount £	Debit ✓	Credit ✓

Select your entries for the 'Account name' column from the following list: Discounts allowed, Irrecoverable debt expense, Payables ledger control account, Receivables ledger control account, VAT control account

Mock Assessment Questions

Task 6 (10 marks)

This task is about using the journal to correct errors.

This task contains tasks (a) to (c)

(a) Identify which TWO of the following statements about suspense accounts are true. (2 marks)

	✓
If the trial balance balances, a suspense account will not be required.	
If the trial balance does not balance, it may not be necessary to include a suspense account in the trial balance.	
If errors are not resolved, it is normal practice to include the suspense account in the final accounts	
If a transaction value recorded in one ledger account was transposed, this will result in the need for a suspense account in the trial balance.	

(b) Identify whether each of the errors described below would or would not be disclosed in the trial balance. (2 marks)

Error	Disclosed ✓	Not disclosed ✓
Nihal purchased some stationery, using personal cash and forgot to make a petty cash claim for a reimbursement of the cost.		
Alex did not update the payables ledger account of ABC Ltd for goods purchased in the current month. The payables ledger control account has been updated.		

(c) (i)

| £ 3,306 | Debit |

(c) (ii)

Date: 30 June	Journal to correct error 1		
Account name	Amount £	Debit ✓	Credit ✓
Purchases	3,396	✓	
Suspense	3,396		✓

Date: 30 June	Journal to correct error 2		
Account name	Amount £	Debit ✓	Credit ✓
Suspense	90	✓	
Repairs	90		✓

Mock Assessment Questions

Task 7 (10 marks)

This task is about extracting the trial balance.

This task contains tasks (a) to (b).

Blake runs a shop. Most of the ledgers have been closed off and the balances included in the trial balance as at 30 November.

(a) Complete the remaining ledger accounts by inserting the balance carried down on each account. Enter your answers to two decimal points. (4 marks)

VAT control

Details	Amount £	Details	Amount £
Purchases	8,752.91	Balance b/d	323.44
		Sales	10,453.89
Balance c/d			

Receivables ledger control

Details	Amount £	Details	Amount £
Balance b/d	48,135.79	Bank	44,445.77
Sales	53,682.45	Discount allowed	100.00
		Sales returns	350.00
		Balance c/d	

Bank

Details	Amount £	Details	Amount £
Receivables ledger control	44,445.77	Balance b/d	3,343.18
		Payables ledger control	43,764.55
Balance c/d		HMRC	14,287.38

PRINCIPLES OF BOOKKEEPING CONTROLS

Purchases

Details	Amount £	Details	Amount £
Balance b/d	18,545.77		
Payables ledger control	36,470.45		
Petty cash	369.24	Balance c/d	

(b) Complete the remaining ledger accounts by inserting the balance carried down on each account. Enter your answers to two decimal points. **(6 marks)**

Account name	Debit £	Credit £
Capital		9,121.14
Bank		
Wages expense	13,731.86	
Purchases		
Sales		66,909.51
VAT control		
Receivables ledger control		
Payables ledger control		35,011.20
Fixtures and fittings	2,250.00	
Heat and light	1,725.82	

Mock Assessment Questions

Task 8 (10 marks)

This task is about redrafting a trial balance.

The initial list of balances for Rhys's business at 31 December is:

Account name	£
Purchases	13,859.21
Payables ledger control account	10,345.38
Plant and equipment	4,840.43
Capital account	15,874.35
Discounts allowed	230.15
Receivables ledger control	16,423.18
Sales	20,025.02
Bank	7,945.27

Some errors have been identified and the following journals are required to be posted:

Date: 31 December	Journal item 1		
Account name	Amount £	Debit ✓	Credit ✓
Plant and equipment	3,000.00	✓	
Suspense	3,000.00		✓
Date: 31 December	Journal item 2		
Account name	Amount £	Debit ✓	Credit ✓
Suspense	53.49	✓	
Purchases	53.49		✓

PRINCIPLES OF BOOKKEEPING CONTROLS

Complete the adjusted trial balance by inserting the correct figures in either the debit or credit column and entering totals for each column.

(10 marks)

Account name	Debit £	Credit £
Purchases		
Payables ledger control account		
Plant and equipment		
Capital account		
Discounts allowed		
Receivables ledger control		
Sales		
Bank		
Total		

Mock Assessment Questions

PRINCIPLES OF BOOKKEEPING CONTROLS

2 Mock Assessment Answers

Task 1

(a) Identify which ONE of the following is correct in relation to the receivables ledger control account. **(1 mark)**

A receivables ledger control account should always be produced by the same person who produces the subsidiary ledgers as this improves accuracy.	
A receivables ledger control account enables discrepancies between the bank and the subsidiary ledger to be quickly identified.	
A receivables ledger control account enables quick identification of the total amount owed to the business by customers.	✓
A receivables ledger control account enables quick identification of an amount owed by a particular customer.	

(b) **(8 marks)**

VAT Control Account

Details	Amount £	Details	Amount £
		Balance b/d	4,650
Purchases	6,927	Sales	10,760
Sales returns	156	Purchases returns	96
Discounts allowed	24	Discounts received	36
Bank	5,115	Cash sales	3,180
Balance c/d	6,500		

Mock Assessment Answers

(c) **(1 mark)**

Payables ledger control account

Details	Amount £	Details	Amount £
Purchases returns	1,230	Balance b/d	13,452
Bank	33,692	Purchases	53,478
Discounts received	420		
Balance c/d	31,588		

Task 2

(a) Identify which ONE of the following statements is a reason for completing this reconciliation. **(1 mark)**

Any errors identified can be identified and included in the suspense account balance to investigate and resolve.	
The payables ledger can be deleted once it has been reconciled which helps to keep record keeping simple.	
Errors in either the payables ledger control account or the payables ledger can be identified and corrected.	✓
The payables ledger control account is always more accurate than the payables ledger.	

(b) (i) If the receivables ledger control balance reconciles with the receivables ledger, what will be the balance? **(2 marks)**

£ 62,109

The balance on the receivables ledger control account is £62,380.

(b) (ii) Complete the following statement **(2 marks)**

The receivables ledger is £271 LOWER than the receivables ledger control account.

PRINCIPLES OF BOOKKEEPING CONTROLS

(c) Identify whether each of the following may explain differences between the two balances (5 marks)

Reason	May explain the difference	Does not explain the difference
An individual ledger account balance was included twice in the total of payables ledger balances.		✓
Early settlement discount received was omitted from the payables ledger control account.	✓	
A cash purchase has not been recorded in the accounting records.		✓
An individual ledger account balance was omitted from the list of payables ledger account balances when it was totalled.	✓	
A transposition error was made when recording a purchase in the purchases daybook.		✓

Task 3

(a) Insert ONE payment method for each description into the space provided. (4 marks)

A plastic card issued by a bank that permits the account holder to purchase goods and services on credit.	Credit card
An electronic system used to make payments from one bank account to another, mainly used for direct debits and credits, with transfers normally taking up to three working days.	BACS
A regular payment of the same amount that is paid on a specified date.	Standing order
A plastic card issued by a bank allowing the account holder to transfer money electronically from their bank account when making a purchase of goods or services.	Debit card

Mock Assessment Answers

(b) Identify which ONE of the following statements is true **(1 mark)**

Statement	
The balance on the bank statement will always be the same as the cash book balance.	
An overdrawn balance of £750 on the bank statement would be equivalent to a credit balance of £750 in the cash book.	✓
There are never errors in the transactions recorded on the bank statement.	

(c) Identify whether each of the following statements is true or false
(3 marks)

Statement	True	False
Transactions which are not yet recorded in the cash book are examples of timing differences.		✓
Comparing the debit side of the cash book to the amounts paid in per the bank statement will enable any automated receipts that have been missed in the cash book to be identified	✓	
The cash book should not include payments made by direct debit or standing order.		✓

PRINCIPLES OF BOOKKEEPING CONTROLS

Task 4

Update the cash book, calculate the closing balance, and then prepare a bank reconciliation at 30 June **(12 marks)**

Date 20X7	Details	Bank £	Date 20X7	Chq No	Details	Bank £
1 June	Balance b/f	12,000	2 June	11231	Ally & Co	2,131
22 June	A Dude	300	2 June	11232	Mr Wong	123
23 June	XPT Ltd	1,500	2 June	11233	Nina's Supplies	892
23 June	Marks Bros	2,150	2 June	11234	Bits & Bobs	2,141
7 June	Wright Bros	1,532	8 June	11235	PPP Ltd	212
			18 June	11236	Mama's Materials	2,350
			20 June	–	Aldo Insurers	900
			22 June	11237	George Richards	5,000
			14 June		Pink Panther	531
			21 June		Bank charges	20
			22 June		Overdraft fee	15
					Balance c/d	3,167
		17,482				17,482
1 July	Balance b/d	3,167				

Mock Assessment Answers

Bank reconciliation statement	£
Balance per bank statement	6,867
Outstanding lodgements	
XPT Ltd	1,500
Wright Bros	2,150
Total outstanding lodgements	3,650
Unpresented cheques	
Mama's Materials	2,350
George Richards	5,000
Total unpresented cheques	7,350
Balance as per cash book	3,167

Task 5

(a) Identify which TWO of the following situations would be a correct use of the journal. **(2 marks)**

Akira identified that a credit sale transaction was recorded twice in the sales day book. Akira will correct this by recording the adjustment in the journal.	✓
Bao paid for some office cleaning materials from petty cash and has recorded this transaction in the journal.	
Nimay wanted to record a contra between the payables ledger control account and the receivables ledger control account. Nimay recorded this transaction in the journal.	✓
Amory recorded prompt payment discount received from a supplier in the journal.	

PRINCIPLES OF BOOKKEEPING CONTROLS

(b) After the journals are processed, what will be the revised balance on the Payroll Liabilities - HMRC account? **(2 marks)**

Payroll liabilities – HMRC account

Details	Amount £	Details	Amount £
		Balance b/d	128
		Nat ins - employer	2,570
		Nat ins - employee	3,028
Balance c/d	9,027	PAYE	3,301

(c) Complete the journal entries below to record the irrecoverable debt write off in the general ledger. You should select the account name from the picklist and then include the appropriate amount in either the Debit or Credit column of the journal entry. **(6 marks)**

Account name	Amount £	Debit ✓	Credit ✓
Receivables ledger control account	525.00		✓
VAT control account	87.50	✓	
Irrecoverable debt expense	437.50	✓	

Task 6

(a) Identify which TWO of the following statements about suspense accounts are true. **(2 marks)**

If the trial balance is in balance, a suspense account will not be required.	✓
If the trial balance does not balance, it may not be necessary to include a suspense account in the trial balance.	
If errors are not resolved, it is normal practice to include the suspense account in the final accounts	
If a transaction value recorded in one ledger account was transposed, this will result in the need for a suspense account in the trial balance.	✓

Mock Assessment Answers

(b) Identify whether each of the errors described below would or would not be disclosed in the trial balance. **(2 marks)**

Error	Disclosed ✓	Not disclosed ✓
Nihal purchased some stationery, using personal cash and forgot to make a petty cash claim for a reimbursement of the cost.		✓
Alex did not update the payables ledger account of ABC Ltd for goods purchased in the current month. The payables ledger control account has been updated.		✓

(c) (i) What is the balance on the suspense account in the trial balance? **(2 marks)**

£	3,306	Debit	*Delete which does not apply

Suspense Account

Details		Amount £	Details	Amount £
Total debits		40,456	Total credits	43,762
Balance b/d		3,306	Nat ins – employer	2,570

PRINCIPLES OF BOOKKEEPING CONTROLS

(c) (ii) Complete the table below to show the debits and credits that will be processed to clear the suspense account.

(4 marks)

Date: 30 June	Journal to correct error 1		
Account name	Amount £	Debit ✓	Credit ✓
Purchases	3,396	✓	
Suspense	3,396		✓
Date: 30 June	Journal to correct error 2		
Account name	Amount £	Debit ✓	Credit ✓
Suspense	90	✓	
Repairs	90		✓

Task 7

(a) Complete the remaining ledger accounts by inserting the balance carried down on each account. Enter your answers to two decimal points.

(4 marks)

VAT control

Details	Amount £	Details	Amount £
Purchases	8,752.91	Balance b/d	323.44
		Sales	10,453.89
Balance c/d	2,024.42		

Receivables ledger control

Details	Amount £	Details	Amount £
Balance b/d	48,135.79	Bank	44,445.77
Sales	53,682.45	Discount allowed	100.00
		Sales returns	350.00
		Balance c/d	56,922.47

Mock Assessment Answers

Bank

Details	Amount £	Details	Amount £
Receivables ledger control	44,445.77	Balance b/d	3,343.18
		Payables ledger control	43,764.55
Balance c/d	16,949.34	HMRC	14,287.38

Purchases

Details	Amount £	Details	Amount £
Balance b/d	18,545.77		
Payables ledger control	36,470.45		
Petty cash	369.24	Balance c/d	55,385.46

(b) Complete the remaining ledger accounts by inserting the balance carried down on each account. Enter your answers to two decimal points. **(6 marks)**

Account name	Debit £	Credit £
Capital		9,121.14
Bank		16,949.34
Wages expense	13,731.86	
Purchases	55,385.46	
Sales		66,909.51
VAT control		2,024.42
Receivables ledger control	56,922.47	
Payables ledger control		35,011.20
Fixtures and fittings	2,250.00	
Heat and light	1,725.82	
Totals	130,015.61	130,015.61

Task 8

Complete the adjusted trial balance by inserting the correct figures in either the debit or credit column and entering totals for each column.

(10 marks)

Account name	Debit £	Credit £
Purchases	13,805.72	
Payables ledger control account		10,345.38
Plant and equipment	7,840.43	
Capital account		15,874.35
Discounts allowed	230.15	
Receivables ledger control	16,423.18	
Sales		20,025.02
Bank	7,945.27	
Total	46,244.75	46,244.75

Mock Assessment Answers

Appendix 1 – International accounting terminology and the alternatives

AAT Q2022

Accounting terminology used in Kaplan learning materials

The Kaplan AAT Q2022 publications and related learning materials employ a range of terminology, in addition to the international accounting terminology used by AAT in its final unit specifications.

The mocks within our Study Texts and Exam Kits use terminology consistent with that in the AAT unit specifications.

This approach is adopted for the following reasons:

1. it aids and supports understanding of terminology and principles relevant to learners not only in their AAT studies but also throughout their practical training and employment

2. it aids and supports understanding by learners of their workplace activities where a range of terminology is used, or may be used, as and when they join the workforce

3. it aids learners throughout their studies, particularly those who commenced their studies under AQ2016 and are continuing under Q2022, or have transferred their studies from another training provider

4. our learning materials are written by expert tutors whose experience it is that learners do value this approach as it helps to provide clarification and understanding

5. it is also important for learners to know what they will encounter in their live assessments.

Many AAT learners will also be training as apprentices. Apprenticeship programmes require learners to develop appropriate technical knowledge, alongside work-relevant skills such as effective communication. Exposure to a range of terminology will help to support learners to develop this understanding of the different terminology used in their studies, their workplaces and in their everyday life, including in the press and media.

Appendix 1: International accounting terminology and the alternatives

Examples

Examples of alternative terminology used in the news media include a BBC website item on the balance sheets of Irish banks on 18 January 2022, and, on 21 January 2022, it had an item on surplus Amazon stock being given away. The Times reported on a business collapse on 10 January 2022 with reference to its creditors and many other similar uses of alternative terminology in the news could be highlighted.

Alternative terminology is regularly used in recruitment adverts for job opportunities. Here are some recent examples:

'……are currently recruiting for the position of a Purchase Ledger Supervisor who will be based at our office in ….. The role is responsible for supervising a Purchase ledger team of 5….'

'We are looking for a Finance Administrator to assist with processing and inputting information in payroll and maintaining the purchase ledger. Finance Administrator responsibilities include….'

'An excellent opportunity to join a multibillion turnover, Global Leader in the automotive sector as a Purchase Ledger Clerk. You will utilise your skills in Accounting and Finance to work alongside this high performing accounts team. As you continue to enhance your skills development to senior and lead positions within the department will be available….You will be an integral part of the accounts team leading the way on multicurrency ERP systems.'

Within the Kaplan UK finance function, there are further examples of occupied posts. There is, for example, a 'Sales Ledger Assistant' and a 'Sales Ledger Manager'.

During your working life you will encounter a range of accounting terminology, and this will continue to evolve. A transfer to another department in the workplace, or a move to a new employer may well expose you to different terminology. Communicating with non-accountants in the workplace may also mean that you have to understand the alternatives that others are familiar with.

PRINCIPLES OF BOOKKEEPING CONTROLS

Activities

We have prepared a glossary of terms which maps this alternative terminology that is used on occasion in Kaplan's learning materials[1].

In many cases, the relevant study text includes a statement highlighting both the international accounting standards terminology used by AAT in its assessments and the equivalent alternatives.

Why not add the definitions of these terms to the glossary below as a reminder when you come across the alternative terminology in the workplace or in your everyday life that it has exactly the same meaning.

Then test your knowledge of accounting terminology with our crossword and "match the terms" activities.

Appendix 1: International accounting terminology and the alternatives

Glossary of terms

International accounting standards terminology	Alternative terminology	Complete the table by adding a definition
Inventory	Stock	
Non-current assets	Fixed assets	
Payable	Creditor	
Payables ledger	Purchases ledger Creditors ledger	
Payables ledger control account (PLCA)	Purchases ledger control account (PLCA) Creditors ledger control account (CLCA)	

PRINCIPLES OF BOOKKEEPING CONTROLS

Receivable	Debtor	
Receivables ledger	Sales ledger Debtors ledger	
Receivables ledger control account (RLCA)	Sales ledger control account (SLCA) Debtors ledger control account (DLCA)	
Allowance for doubtful receivables Allowance for doubtful debts	Doubtful debt provision	
Statement of financial position	Balance sheet	
Statement of profit or loss	Income statement	

Appendix 1: International accounting terminology and the alternatives

Accounting Crossword

Test your knowledge of accounting terminology with the following crossword. The answers contain a mixture of international accounting standards terminology and some alternatives.

Across:

3   An international accounting standards word used to describe an amount due to the business from a customer. (10)

6   How would amounts held in a bank current account be presented in the statement of financial position? (7,5)

8   A bank loan due for repayment in five years is an example of this type of liability. (3-7)

10 An example of a non-current asset. (4)

12 If a business owes money to a supplier, it is often referred to as 'a _____ of the business'. (8)

13 'Early _____' discount is another term used for prompt payment discount. (10)

PRINCIPLES OF BOOKKEEPING CONTROLS

Down:

1 A word traditionally used to describe an amount due to the business from a customer. (6)

2 An amount introduced into the business by the owner. (7)

4 An estimate of an expense incurred but not yet paid. (7)

5 Another word for goods held for resale. (9)

7 Double entry bookkeeping consists of 'debits and _____'. (7)

9 The document produced by a business when it has sold goods to a customer on credit which is then recorded in a daybook. (7)

11 '_____ discount' is a term used to describe a reduction in the unit price of goods sold due to the quantity purchased by the customer. (5)

Match the terms

Test your knowledge of accounting terminology by finding a matching term for each item in the first column. Make your selection from the available options in the final column. The activity contains a mixture of international accounting standards terminology and some alternatives.

Term	Match	Options
Bad debt		Long-term liability
Doubtful debt provision		Value added tax
Equity		Sole proprietor
Fixed asset		Early settlement discount
Non-current liability		Capital
Prompt payment discount		Irrecoverable debt
Sales tax		Allowance for receivables
Sole trader		Non-current asset

Appendix 1: International accounting terminology and the alternatives

Solutions

Accounting crossword

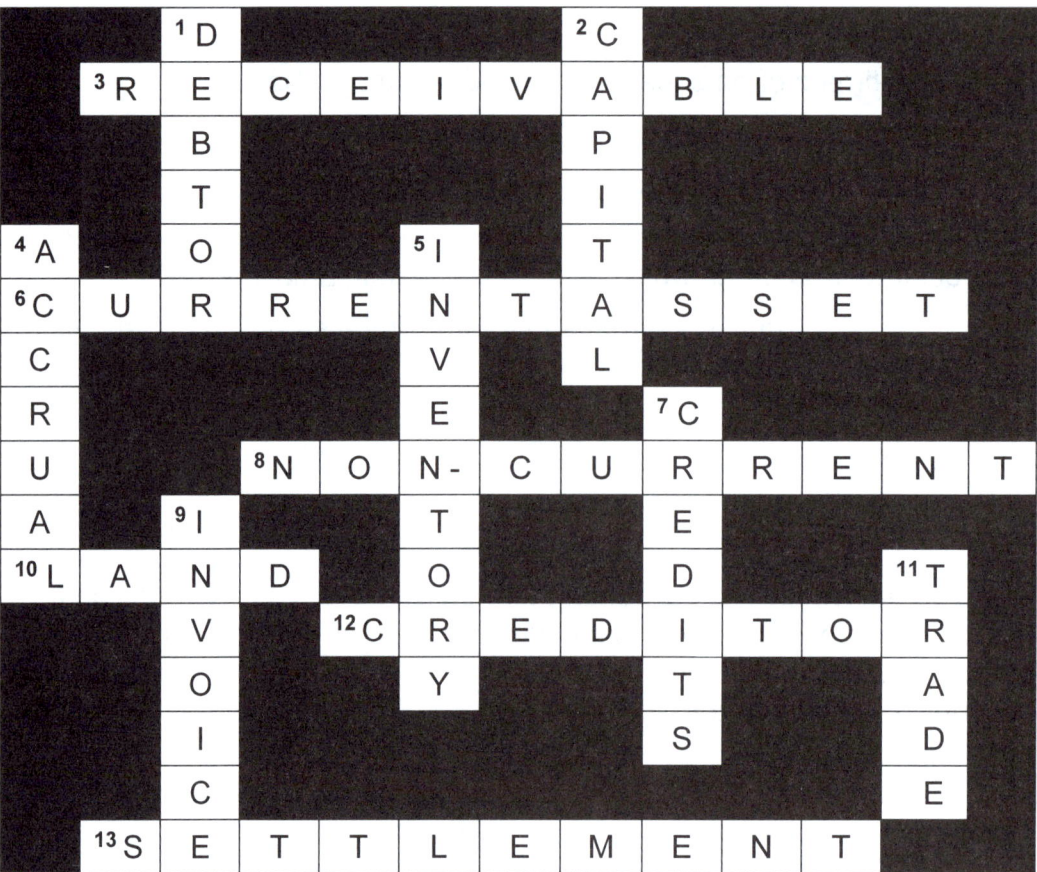

PRINCIPLES OF BOOKKEEPING CONTROLS

Match the terms

Term	Match
Bad debt	Irrecoverable debt
Doubtful debt provision	Allowance for receivables
Equity	Capital
Fixed asset	Non-current asset
Non-current liability	Long-term liability
Prompt payment discount	Early settlement discount
Sales tax	Value added tax
Sole trader	Sole proprietor

Appendix 1: International accounting terminology and the alternatives

Add your own notes below as you encounter uses of international accounting standards terminology and their alternatives

INDEX

A

Accounting equation, 3
Adjusted trial balance, 29
Asset, 3

B

BACS (Bankers Automated Clearing System), 150, 152
Bad debt(s), 64, 68, 94
    expense, 64
Balancing, 21
Bank, 13, 14, 15, 16, 17, 18, 19, 21, 25, 27, 28, 31, 44, 49, 50, 51, 52
    account, 140
    reconciliation, 137, 152
    reconciliation – step by step procedure, 153
    statement, 152
Banking system, 137
Bonuses, 121

C

Capital, 3
Cash, 1, 2, 10, 14, 15, 16, 21, 23, 34, 60
    book, 58, 137, 138, 152
    payments book, 138
    receipts book, 138
Casting error, 94
CHAPS (Clearing House Automated Payments System)., 151
Cheques, 142, 143, 144
Clock card, 120
Commission, 121
Compensating error, 95
Contra entry, 60, 65, 75
Credit, 1, 2, 10, 14, 15, 16, 17, 19, 20, 23, 24, 28, 29, 30, 34, 36, 43
    transactions, 17
Creditor(s), 74, 139
Current
    assets, 3
    liabilities, 4

D

DEAD CLIC, 10
Debit, 29, 30, 31
    cards, 165
Debtor(s), 58, 140
Direct debits, 148, 152
Discounts, 58
    allowed, 60
    received, 74
Double entry, 1, 13, 24, 25, 28, 36
Double entry bookkeeping, 59
    the principles of, 2
Drawee, 141
Drawings, 26
Dual effect, 2

E

Error(s), 70, 93, 109
    correction of, 96
    of commission, 95
    of omission, 95
    of principle, 95
Extraction error, 95

G

Gross pay, 117, 118, 120
Gross pay, 118

I

Income tax, 117, 118, 122

J

Journal, 12, 57, 68
Journal, 57
Journal, 68

Index

L

Ledger, 2, 14, 17, 21, 23, 24, 25, 29, 34
    account, 1
    accounting – opening balances, 68
Liability, 3

M

Main ledger, 60, 74

N

National insurance contributions (NIC), 117, 118, 123
    employees', 124
    employer's, 124
Non-current
    assets, 3
    liabilities, 4

O

Omission error, 95
Omissions, 93
Overtime, 121

P

Pay As You Earn (PAYE), 118, 122
Payee, 141
Payroll
    accounting procedures, 117, 127
    confidentiality, 119
    deductions, 118
    function – overview, 118
    statutory deductions, 125
    Pension contributions, 119
Personal allowance, 122
Profit, 3
Purchase invoice, 74
Purchases, 15, 16, 18, 19, 21, 26, 27, 28, 31, 40, 41, 44, 49, 52, 75
    credit, 74
    day book, 74
Purchases ledger, 74, 76, 77
    control account, 74, 76
    control account reconciliation, 76
Purchases returns, 26, 27
    day book, 74, 75

S

Sales, 16, 18, 19, 21, 26, 27, 28, 31, 40, 41, 44, 49, 50, 51, 52, 60
    credit, 58
    day book, 58, 60
Sales ledger, 58, 60, 67
    control account, 58, 60, 64, 67
    control account reconciliation, 67, 70
Sales returns, 26, 60
    day book, 58
Separate entity concept, 2
Single entry, 94
Standing order(s), 148, 152
Statement of financial position, 4
Statutory maternity pay (SMP), 120, 122
Statutory sick pay (SSP), 120, 122
Subsidiary ledger, 69
Suspense account, 93, 97, 109
    clearing of, 99

T

Timesheets, 121
Transposition error, 70
Transposition error, 95
Trial balance, 24, 28, 44, 52, 93, 94, 95, 98, 109
    errors detected by, 94
    errors not detected by, 95
    re-drafting of, 105

V

VAT, 65

W

Wages and salaries, 117, 119, 120